AMERICA'S FORGOTTEN
LABOR ORGANIZATION

A Survey of the Role of the
Single-Firm Independent Union
in American Industry

America's Forgotten Labor Organization

A Survey of the Role of the Single-Firm Independent Union in American Industry

BY

ARTHUR B. SHOSTAK

Department of Sociology
University of Pennsylvania
and formerly on
Research Staff of the
Industrial Relations Section

1962
INDUSTRIAL RELATIONS SECTION
Department of Economics
PRINCETON UNIVERSITY
Princeton, New Jersey, U.S.A.

HD
L490
I6
S47

INDUSTRIAL RELATIONS SECTION
Department of Economics
PRINCETON UNIVERSITY
Princeton, New Jersey, U.S.A.

FREDERICK HARBISON, *Director*
HAZEL BENJAMIN, *Librarian*
NELLIE OFFUTT, *Administrative Assistant*
DORIS McBRIDE, *Secretary*

WILLIAM G. BOWEN, *Faculty Associate*
J. DOUGLAS BROWN, *Faculty Associate*
RICHARD A. LESTER, *Faculty Associate*
WILBERT E. MOORE, *Faculty Associate*

The reports of the Industrial Relations Section are the joint product of the Section's staff under the supervision of the Director. In the case of each report, the research and preparation of manuscript is done by the staff member whose name appears on the title page.

Research Report Series No. 103

FOREWORD

THE American system of organized labor comprises a wide variety of institutions. There are international unions affiliated with the central federation—the AFL-CIO. There are other strong internationals, such as the United Mine Workers and some of the Railroad Brotherhoods, which are unaffiliated with a central body. There are local unions which are affiliated with the AFL-CIO, and finally, there are independent unions, affiliated with neither the internationals nor the AFL-CIO, which bargain for the most part with single enterprises. These latter institutions, referred to in this study as "single-firm independent unions," are in many respects America's forgotten labor organizations in that they have received very little attention in the published literature on contemporary industrial relations. Dr. Shostak's study is designed to fill this rather significant gap in our knowledge of the labor movement in the United States.

In this volume, Dr. Shostak examines the different "personalities" of these unions. He compares them with local unions of the internationals. And, he examines critically their role as bargainers within the system of organized labor. He finds that these unions are more "independent" than is generally recognized, and that they have shown a remarkable capacity to survive despite the hostility of most of the organized labor movement and the indifferent attitudes of employers. He concludes his analysis by setting forth some striking paradoxes. For example, he notes that the weakest independent unions are the most secure within the system of organized labor, while the strongest are the ones in greatest danger of being captured by the internationals. And he suggests that the independent union, which "epitomizes an ideal of Jeffersonian democracy," may be an anachronism in modern industrial relations where the dealings between labor and management are increasingly characterized by consolidations of power on both sides.

This study is based upon two years of intensive research by the author for the Industrial Relations Section. During this period, he examined thoroughly the bits and pieces of available written knowledge, and he conducted extensive interviews

Foreword

with officials of the unions themselves as well as with the employers with whom they had bargaining relationships. Although the field work was confined largely to unions in New Jersey, the study presents, in our judgment, a definitive statement of the nature and role of these unions throughout the country.

The Section wishes to express its thanks for the wholehearted cooperation given to Dr. Shostak by the officers of many independent unions and the officials of two major associations of single-firm unions. Several businessmen and government officials also contributed significantly to the study's candor and scope. Appreciation is also expressed to representatives of the AFL-CIO and the several international unions who responded so freely to the searching questions put to them by Dr. Shostak. Finally, the Section wishes to extend particular thanks to Mrs. Marvin Goldberger of Princeton Editorial Research Associates for her competent assistance in editing the manuscript and her help in the organization and clarification of the major concepts developed by the author.

Frederick Harbison
Director

Princeton, New Jersey
August 15, 1962

AUTHOR'S ACKNOWLEDGMENTS

During the course of my work on this volume, I profited from the guidance of Professors Charles H. Page, Richard A. Lester, and Frederick Harbison of the Princeton University faculty. The Industrial Relations library and the Section's secretarial, administrative and editorial staff rendered invaluable assistance. And finally, my wife Susan lent great moral support and editorial guidance. This study was made possible by the assistance of these men and women, and particularly by union leaders, company executives, and government officials who cooperated so wholeheartedly in providing me with information and ideas. I wish to dedicate this study to my parents whose interest and support was a continuous inspiration. I alone, however, assume responsibility for the ideas and conclusions presented.

CONTENTS

Contents

I. INTRODUCTION: DEFINING THE SINGLE-FIRM INDEPENDENT UNION

A N interested reader has available a large number of books on American labor unions. He can choose from serious academic studies, political tracts, and journalistic exposés, all undertaken from many different points of view. However, even this wealth of material overlooks one particular form of union organization. The single-firm independent union has not been discussed in a general book-length study for 35 years.*

As its name implies, the single-firm independent union confines its membership to the employees of a single employer and remains aloof from international unions and the AFL-CIO. The single-firm union is the dominant form of labor organization in the chemical industry and comes close to being so in the telephone and petroleum industries. The Bureau of Labor Statistics estimates there may be as many as 1,400 single-firm unions with a total membership of 400,000 workers spread throughout the 50 states.[1] (The union is also found in Canada, Indonesia, Israel, Japan, and elsewhere.)[2]

With a history that stretches back almost to the turn of the century, the single-firm union is no newcomer to the American labor scene. However, as a consequence of some black pages in its background and a lack of publicity in recent years, the contemporary independent is a victim of widespread confusion. Some mistakenly identify the independent single-firm union with small racketeer-dominated "independent unions." But such nefarious organizations are almost never confined to a single employer's employees; racketeer unions must include many firms to satisfy greedy leaders. The independent union is often identified as a holdover of the employer-dominated company union of the 1930's. But significant changes have occurred in industrial relations over the last thirty years and no union is now actually supported by management. Finally, some insist the union is not a union at all. It is plain that its unusual brand of unionism disappoints those who envision

* The last such book was Robert Dubin's *Company Unions: Employers 'Industrial Democracy'* (New York: Vanguard Press, 1927).

1

Introduction

unions as a vehicle of social protest, a businesslike seller of labor, or a source of personal power. However, the single-firm union offers blue- and white-collar workers much of what they want in a union and their definition of unionism must command attention and respect.

Background. The single-firm independent union has its origin in two management tools, shop committees and employee representation plans. Introduced in the early 1900's by such men as Filine, Leitch, and Rockefeller, Jr., the committees and plans were confined to the employees of a single employer and remained independent of international unions and of the AFL. The committees and plans, however, were not labor organizations, but techniques of personnel administration and adjuncts of the personnel department. As such they generally avoided action on real bread and butter issues in favor of action on relatively minor items. A worker summed up his years of frustration with a famous plan with these words:

> "They were able to get new soap containers in the shower baths but no soap."[3]

Professor Irving Bernstein of the University of California, looking back from the vantage point of 1960, notes the lack of a single recorded case of a plan that grew into a genuine union during the twenties.[4] On the other hand, "employers and workers alike became accustomed to the need for organization in shop relations."[5]

Unlike the committees and plans, the company unions of the 1930's were avowed labor organizations. Unfortunately they were usually employer-sponsored and employer-dominated, a fact which continues to haunt contemporary single-firm unions. Indeed, their betrayal of workers coerced or duped into membership was so severe that one student of labor unions, Father William J. Smith, now believes:

> "The very name 'Company Union' is a stench in the nostrils of every bona fide, red-blooded union man. It carries with it an age-old stigma of sniffling servitude, of despicable labor spies, of damnable discriminations, of social and economic bondage, of frustrated attempts at justice, of

Introduction

starvation wages, of inhuman working conditions, of sabotaged strikes and in some instances, machine guns, tear-gas bombs, and threatening bayonets."[6]

Without denying this, it is also important to recognize that company unions offered members local autonomy, low dues, industrial harmony, competitive labor contracts, and the endorsement of employers who valued the flexibility of dealing solely with their own employees. By 1935 there were more than 2,000,000 members in company unions, the largest bloc ever to organize outside of the international unions.[7]

In 1935 the National Labor Relations Act (the Wagner Act) expressly prohibited employers from dominating labor unions. Two years later the Supreme Court upheld the constitutionality of the Act and the company union movement ground to a halt. Most of the unions proved to have been training grounds for legitimate unionism and they were quickly converted into locals of aggressive international organizations. A few disbanded and left behind unorganized (and often disorganized) shops. Some adapted themselves to the new law and environment and continue to exist today in the form of vigorous militant single-firm unions.

As far as the average citizen is concerned, however, there are only three types of trade union: legitimate (most locals of most international unions), suspicious (some locals of some international unions), and employer-dominated company unions (all past and present single-firm independent unions). In the case of the single-firm union, the association has sound historical roots. That is, the public had its most intense contact with this type of union during its peak years in the 1930's, years marked by nefarious employer activities. The limelight was by no means flattering. Thus, misapprehension about single-firm unions arises from their history, but the resulting stigma, now 25 years old and still powerful, undermines the morale of members and hinders the spread of the unions into unorganized plants.

Growth. From a peak membership of 2,000,000 in company unions in the mid-thirties the single-firm union has fallen to about 400,000 members. Similarly, the uncounted thousands of

3

Introduction

company unions thirty years ago have as descendants only about 1,400 independent single-firm unions. Much of the decline took place soon after the Court upheld the Wagner Act in 1937 and the international unions and the new NLRB began critical examinations of the single-firm unions. Unfortunately, it is not possible to say with any exactness how numbers have changed since that time. The evidence in the matter is confusing and suspect. For one thing, the most thorough survey conducted in the 1950's, a survey of the Wage Stabilization Board, appears to have included multi-firm along with single-firm independent unions.[8] For another, federal surveys sometimes exclude and sometimes include small unions that fall outside federal jurisdiction. State surveys are few and far between.[9]

In any case, available data suggests a slight decline over the last decade in the national population of single-firm unions along with a sharp increase in the population of certain states. The Wage Stabilization Board located 2,607 single-firm (and multi-firm) organizations in 1952; the Bureau of Labor Statistics found only 1,400 single-firm unions in 1961. On the other hand, New York State counted 95 single-firm (and possibly some multi-firm) unions in 1950, almost 200 in 1955, and 248 in 1960. Similarly, the New Jersey total has grown from 37 in 1942 to 95 in 1961.

Distribution. It is possible to trace the industrial, geographic, and membership distribution of independent unions with some assurance. It appears that the single-firm unions are concentrated in public utilities and the metal, petroleum, chemical and telephone industries, but have substantial numbers only in the latter three industries. Similarly, although they can be found in all 50 states, they have always been concentrated in the North Eastern and North Central states. The majority have less than 500 members; larger single-firm unions are found mainly in refineries, chemical plants and telephone companies.

The industrial distribution of single-firm independent unions points up their absence in two major types of industry: those characterized by movement from job to job inside the industry such as construction or mining and those characterized by a history of joint action on labor contracts by many employers

4

Introduction

such as the steel and automobile industries. Since these unions restrict their memberships to the employees of a single employer, they are not suited for industries which involve transfer cards and union hiring halls, or industries marked by multi-employer contracts or industry-wide bargaining. This constitutes a restriction on the development of the union that does not apply to rival international organizations.

This distribution also indicates other characteristics of the industries where the single-firm union is commonly found. The industries are led by business giants. These giants dwarf the single-firm unions and command more resources than do the unions. The industries consider labor costs only a small part of total costs; dealings between labor and management are thus robbed of economic urgency from the employer's point of view. As labor costs are relatively minor the industries have long paid special attention to ample programs of paternalistic benefits. These benefits are vital in the independent union's struggle to persist in the face of raids and rivalry from international unions. Finally, the industries are marked by continuous-flow operations, the kind that lend themselves readily to automation. This in turn dulls the effectiveness of the strike as a union tool and strengthens the employer's already strong hand.

The geographic distribution of the single-firm independent union points up their absence in the South, the last stronghold of the open shop. This absence lends support to the notion that single-firm unions appear most often today as a buffer against the international unions. In the same vein the long-time presence of the single-firm unions in the North Central and North Eastern states makes it plain that the union is no hot-house product. It has persisted in fighting range of international union rivals for decades.

The distribution of the unions by size is apparently biased in favor of companies with a small number of employees, or, more often, with many scattered plants of relatively few workers. Not only are the international unions reluctant to undertake the expense of representing such locations, but the character of the single-firm independent union lends itself to the family atmosphere of many small workshops. However, the existence of single-firm unions with several thousand members

Introduction

shows that it can also survive in a less congenial atmosphere marked by intense competition from international unions.

Perspective. In the years that have passed since the rise and fall of the company union, the nation's single-firm unions have undergone considerable change. Many single-firm unions have developed into strong organizations, fully the equal of active locals of major unions. Some have attempted to form associations to further strengthen one another. A few have appeared among office workers and among professional engineers. What is significant, in short, is that time has witnessed the appearance of *diversity* and even *experimentation* in the universe of single-firm unions. Much of this is in direct response to lessons contained in the union's background.

While a discussion of this background fills in much material, it also raises many questions. In the chapters that follow the general character of the unions will be outlined and the effects of different types of membership on this character will be examined. The single-firm unions will be compared in detail with local unions and their relationship will be examined for clues to the persistence of the single-firm organization. An explanation will be offered for the disappointing performance of associations of single-firm unions, and the study will conclude with a discussion of the likely future of America's forgotten labor organization. Time and again the study will call attention back to some facet of the union's background, for the single-firm independent union is especially a product, and peculiarly a victim, of its past.

FOOTNOTES

1. See Bureau of Labor Statistics, *Unaffiliated Local and Single-Employer Unions in the United States, 1961* (Washington, D.C.: Government Printing Office, forthcoming).

2. See Department of Labor, *Labour Organizations in Canada, 1960* (Ottawa, Canada: Economics and Research Branch, Department of Labour, 1960); Goldberg, Harry, "Trade Union Organization and Labor Relations in Indonesia: A Case Study," *American Labor's Role in Less Developed Countries* (Ithaca, New York: New York State School of Industrial and Labor Relations, 1958), p. 61; Ganguli, H. C., "Attitudes of Union and Non-Union Employees in a Calcutta Engineering Factory," *Journal of Applied Psychology*, 40 (1956), pp. 78-82; Tabb, J. Y.; Ami, Y.; and Shaal, O., *Industrial Relations in Israel* (Hebrew), (Tel-Aviv, Israel: Dvir Co., 1961).

6

Introduction

3. Brooks, Robert R. R., *As Steel Goes: Unionism in a Basic Industry* (New Haven, Conn.: Yale University Press, 1940), p. 87.

4. Bernstein, Irving, *The Lean Years: A History of the American Worker: 1920-1933* (Boston, Mass.: Houghton Mifflin Co., 1960), pp. 172, 173.

5. *Ibid.*

6. Smith, William J., S.J., *Spotlight on Labor Unions* (New York: Duell, Sloan and Pearce, 1946), p. 45. Note that the AFL-CIO forbids affiliates to accuse one another of being company unions. However, for an example of just such a use, see Rivers, William L., "The Businesslike Mr. Hoffa," *The Reporter*, February 2, 1961, pp. 28-29.

7. Millis, Harry A. and Royal E. Montgomery, *Organized Labor* (New York: McGraw-Hill, 1945), pp. 837, 841.

8. U. S. Wage Stabilization Board, *Directory of Independent Unions* (Washington, D.C.: WSB, Office of Independent Unions, 1952).

9. See Institute of Labor and Industrial Relations, *Directory of Labor Unions in New Jersey, 1959* (New Brunswick, N.J.: Rutgers University, 1960); New York State Department of Labor, *Directory of Labor Organizations in New York State* (New York: Division of Research and Statistics, Bulletin 233, 1959); Thompson, Kenneth M., "Labor Unions in Louisiana," *Louisiana Business Bulletin*, 21 (September, 1959). Directories of considerably less usefulness include: Department of Industrial Relations, *Union Labor in California, 1959* (San Francisco, Calif.: Division of Labor Statistics and Research, 1960); Nadworny, Milton J., *A Survey of the Labor Movement in Vermont* (Montpelier, Vt.: Vermont Development Commission, 1959); Randa, E. W. and Richardson, R. C., *Union Membership in Utah* (Salt Lake City, Utah: Institute of Industrial Relations, Bulletin 1, 1960).

7

II. PERSONALITY OF THE UNION: AN OVERVIEW

B Y comparing contract terms with Government data it is relatively easy to estimate the economic effectiveness of the single-firm union. Some of these organizations are stronger instruments of collective bargaining than others. Some are more successful in representing the point of view of their members and in reconciling the interests of employee and employer. Overall, however, very few single-firm unions offer members the full variety and degree of economic benefits available in the international unions. It is clear, therefore, that the major reasons for the existence and persistence of single-firm independent unions must be outside the purely economic aspects of these labor organizations.

To understand the single-firm independent unions a knowledge of their contract terms must be supplemented with an examination of their "personality": the core of attitudes members and leaders assume toward the principal union problems and the rationale they offer for these attitudes.[1] No economic study can yield the necessary background; it comes only through the examination of other aspects of union organization.

Although there are some studies of the economic aspects of independent unions no broad-scale study of them has ever been made. In fact, until 1960 when the Landrum-Griffin Act required the filing of information reports by every union* in the United States, the studies necessarily focused on individual independents. No conclusions about the overall characteristics of the independent union could be drawn under the circumstances.

The research on which this work is based began with a close study of the information reports filed by several hundred independent unions with the Bureau of Labor-Management Reports in Washington, D.C. These reports include information on the constitutions and treasuries of the reporting unions.[2] The Bureau of Labor Statistics collection of union contracts was also consulted. Guided by experts in the field of industrial

* Except those unions in plants not engaged in interstate commerce.

8

Union Personality

relations, state and federal officials, businessmen, union officers and other specialists, a list of independent unions was drawn up to reflect the widest possible variety of organizational types.[3]

The core of the research was carried out in a series of intensive two-part interviews by the author with the officers of thirty-six blue-collar and four white-collar single-firm independent unions.[4] The interviews were guided by a questionnaire prepared in advance, but the respondents were not restricted to a discussion of only those topics. The first series of interviews, each lasting about three hours, was carried out in 1960; and a second series using the same respondents was undertaken a year later.[5]

The response from the union officers was generally cooperative, but there was information to be gathered from the hostility of some officers to the questioning. These intensive personal interviews yielded insights into the close similarities in the attitudes of leaders of widely-differing types of independent unions.[6]

The subject matter of the interviews concerned relations between the members of the unions themselves and between the unions and management, the goals of the unions and the methods used to achieve them, and the place and value of independent unionism in the labor movement and the nation as a whole.[7] The remarkable similarity of the opinions expressed on these subjects made it possible to derive a characterization of the independent unions that distinguishes them from other forms of labor organizations: in effect a thumbnail sketch of the "personality" of the independent unions.

Five characteristics appeared in all the unions studied. These characteristics vary little among the unions, although there is wide variation in such matters as age, size, industrial setting, location and even professional status of members.

Each of the 40 organizations was "person-based." It was plant-oriented. It was employer-centered. It was conservative. And it was ideologically-motivated. While individual unions differed in their subscription to any specific characteristic, the five proved integral and therefore, to a large extent, undeniable.

To judge from the interviews and related data, *the single-*

Union Personality

firm union is a person-based organization. As such it relies on interpersonal relations rather than non-personal contacts or material resources. It is also committed to considerable union democracy, both as an intrinsic "good" and as a way of depriving international union critics of a target for criticism. This commitment to democracy means frequent discussions of union affairs during coffee and lunch breaks and considerable reliance on face-to-face relations to direct and sustain the organization. The emphasis, in short, is on people rather than paper, informality rather than formality, the personal touch rather than the procedural route.

What is the significance of the "person-based" characteristic? It promotes an informal and friendly atmosphere. Such bureaucratic elements as strict lines of communication, protocol, designated advancement opportunities and other formalizing procedures are generally replaced by casual, relaxed and personal relationships. It discourages "creeping legalism" and the use of expensive staff aid and encourages self-reliance. Single-firm union leaders take considerable pride in their ability to understand the various labor laws and to secure a profitable labor contract even though many have not completed high school. The "person-based" characteristic helps these unions maintain a highly valued friendship with the employer. The union's informality complements the "one big family" atmosphere encouraged by employers in many small shops. It helps keep union leaders close to fellow workers. Informality abets closeness; there is little distance between the top leader and the least prestigeful follower on the organizational chart, and even less distance in practice. It is possible in many shops to find both working side-by-side on the same machine. Finally, this "personality" characteristic aids union democracy as it makes it easier for losers in union political contests to "return to the bench." They know that their jobs, not their union posts, are the source of their livelihood; and they know the closeness of officers to members minimizes any possible embarrassment over returning to the ranks. This knowledge lessens pressures to compromise democratic ways in order to retain office.

The "person-based" characteristic, like the four others, is not without possible negative effects. For some independent unions

10

Union Personality

an informal and friendly atmosphere weakens the union's ability to discipline its own membership or to adopt a militant pose when advisable. A preference for co-worker as opposed to professional guidance means reliance on poorly prepared and unreliable amateurs. A warm friendship with the employer weakens the union's resolve to champion employee interests. Close relations between leaders and followers undermines the authority of the leaders. And the ease with which losers can "return to the bench" encourages frequent turnover in leadership. Such turnover impedes the development of a corps of skilled and committed officers.

The Single-firm Union is a Plant-oriented Organization. It is primarily concerned with the internal affairs of its own shop and has very little interest in such outside affairs as politics, the public relations efforts of major unions, state and federal welfare legislation and community development. Outside affairs are occasionally discussed informally by co-workers but they fall outside the normal range of these plant-oriented labor unions. Most of these unions are predominantly, if not exclusively, concerned with wages, hours, and working conditions, and with these only in the context of the immediate workplace.

Three explanations were offered by the leaders for the restricted orientation of their unions. Union resources are too limited to spread over both internal and outside affairs. The union is too small and insignificant to influence most outside affairs. And finally some leaders rationalize the focus on the plant by explaining that Big Unions have excessive influence with Big Government. This influence is thought to deny the independent unions a role in politics and to result in various real or imaginary moves against them by extra-plant agents (such as a new NLRB ruling linking single-firm unions with employer-domination). Similarly, this sense of persecution helps explain their reluctance to contact other neighboring labor organizations.

How does this characteristic influence the union? Its plant-orientation limits the "orbit of comparison" used to evaluate contract terms. Many of these unions make little effort to compare their contracts with those at other plants or with con-

11

tract conditions in the area or industry. They thereby lessen the likelihood of disagreement over goals or disappointment with gains. Plant-orientation helps the union direct all its energies to the problems immediately at hand. No part of dues received goes to lobbyists at a distant capital, to distressed workers in another state or to a political candidate in another city. The exclusive focus on shop conditions helps make experts of many leaders and members. They become specialists in the workplace, and they use this specialty to advantage in negotiations. The plant-orientation provides a bond that can unify the membership. Whatever differences the men have among themselves (such as political preference), they are united in a common and exclusive focus on the shop. Finally, the union's plant-orientation helps insure swift, plain, and often profitable negotiations. Management knows discussion will be limited to shop affairs, and both sides prepare and behave accordingly.

Plant-orientation has negative as well as positive effects. In the case of certain unions, ignorance of conditions in other shops gives the employer an unnecessary advantage. The expertise that results from exclusive focus on shop conditions is weakened by lack of comparative data and lack of "backup" resources from friendly unions. The binding nature of a common focus on the shop covers and protects rather than aids the airing and accommodation of serious differences among members. And swift and plain negotiations are not always profitable, especially when one side voluntarily wears "horse-blinders." Ignorance encourages dependency on the employer, a phenomena so suspect as to be officially discouraged in federal labor law.

The Single-firm Union is an Employer-Centered Organization. The energies that other trade unions put into various interests the independent unions put almost exclusively into a close study of the behavior and attitudes of the employer. The independent union is rooted in one shop and its fate is unalterably intertwined with the fate of that shop. The union has no hiring hall, no transfer cards, and no job referral function. If the employer decides to sell the shop, expand or contract the workforce, change his product, automate his plant, or go out of business, the union has little choice but to adjust to the change. As a result, the union hangs on the employer's every move. An inordinate amount of time in the shop is given to the spread and evaluation of rumors covering the employer; unlike talk of politics or sports, this activity has the support and interest of union leaders.

What is the significance of the employer-centered characteristic? A sharp focus on the employer aids the union by helping it counter the employer's full knowledge of its own resources. That is, in the same sense that the union's morale and program are on daily display, so the union profits from a full and close analysis of the employer's profit picture, expansion plans, market position, and the like. A concern with the employer helps many of these unions maintain a close and friendly relationship with management. Union leaders and management representatives deal on a first-name basis; the leaders are career employees and management knows this. Many employers prefer these unions to an international union, and the union leaders know this. The union's focus on the employer, then, helps both parties preserve the union, a goal they often share.

On the other hand, certain of these independent unions are handicapped by their narrow focus on the employer. For some it means excessive concern with his possible reaction to various union moves. The union takes the employer's projected behavior rather than its own best judgment as prescription for action. In this connection, certain unions refrain from joining multi-union associations because an employer might interpret this as a sign of new militancy. Others decline to maintain a strike defense fund because the employer could consider this an aggressive move. A concern with the employer, to the exclusion of other interests common in locals of major unions, makes it difficult for the union to convince skeptics both in and outside of the union that it is independent of the employer and bears little relation to yesteryear's company union. The sharp focus on the employer, in combination with the commitment to industrial harmony, gives rise to suspicions, and occasionally even to accusations of decisive employer influence.

The Single-firm Union is a Conservative Organization. It is inclined to lag rather than lead in the area of ideas and action. It is not particularly imaginative or daring. The union's plant-

Union Personality

orientation also helps here by screening out unsettling ideas developed elsewhere. The single-firm union, in short, does not expect to dazzle anyone with its initiative. Survival is thought sufficient, particularly by the older members who predominate in the common, small workshop. Conservatism is light in its demands on union resources; pioneering or even progressive behavior involves risk-taking that frightens and alienates many members. They prefer the easier route, and this helps explain much of the record of their unions.

What are the consequences of the single-firm union's conservative ways? Many unions gain from the careful husbanding of resources encouraged by conservative behavior. They also profit from membership appreciation of the minimal demands made on them; limited demands for time in meeting, participation on committees, and so forth. Finally, they gain from the likelihood that management is pleased with the union's traditional ideas and action.

On the other hand, the lack of a source of progressive thinking can hamper advisable reforms. For example, regional mores may dictate discriminatory treatment of Negro workers. Those members who believe equalitarian treatment is morally proper or simply necessary to prevent debilitating factionalism are restrained by the union's conservatism. In some cases a low level of demands on the membership results in extreme apathy and disinterest, as well as a loss of confidence in the union's importance in the shop (usually fatal in the case of a plant-oriented organization). Finally, the employer's pleasure with the union's conservatism sometimes leads to similarly conservative bargaining practices on his part. That is, rather than keep the union competitive in contract gains, management trusts to the union's antipathy for "radical outsiders" (such as international union representatives) and "wild-eyed trouble-making ways" (such as a standard work-stoppage) to force union acceptance of an inferior contract.

The Single-firm Union is Committed to an Unusual Ideology. The single-firm independent union possesses an ideology peculiar to itself, one compounded of three related beliefs:

1. The American way is best exemplified by the small enterprise, union or business.

14

Union Personality

2. The small enterprise is the victim of a joint conspiracy of Big Government, Big Business, and Big Labor.
3. The small enterprise could flourish if not for this little-publicized but very effective conspiracy.

Translated into operational terms, the ideology leads the union to admire the small employer it generally deals with and to deprecate the advance of the large impersonal business concern. The union argues that its smallness is less a handicap than a matter of positive choice and a measure of concern with warm, personal, and friendly ways. It does not want to grow large; it champions the Jeffersonian doctrine of small enterprise against the Hamiltonian doctrine of large centralized operations. Such a popularist ideology leads it to suspect that outside agents frustrated by its persistence are busy persecuting it. Many leaders interviewed believe the NLRB has favored the international unions in independent vs. local union contests, and many believe major unions would trade a pledge of a "sweetheart" contract for employer support in a raid on an independent. The ideology supplies a reason to trust in the union's basic effectiveness (dimmed by current persecution) and ultimate promise (possible only when the persecution is lifted). The union is felt to deserve the confidence of its members because of its dramatic identification with the "American way."

Like the four other basic characteristics, this one of ideology can aid or hamper the single-firm independent union. For example, the ideology helps the union explain to members its lack of ties with other unions and its reluctance to participate in extra-shop affairs. It suggests there is something vaguely un-American or at least "less American" about international unions and helps thereby to dampen interest in affiliation. The ideology identifies the independent union with the survival of small employers; and thereby aids union-management relations. For example, it prepares members to occasionally accept poor contract terms when the employer claims he has an emergency. Finally, the ideology contributes two emotional attitudes that help bind the members together: the feeling that they are brave and innocent victims of a conspiracy of more powerful forces,

15

Union Personality

and the feeling that their cause is noble and their "sacrifices" are not in vain. Thus, the union can profit by using the ideology as an excuse for present and future shortcomings (the conspiracy against it) and as a cause "worth fighting for" (Jeffersonian Americanism).

On the other hand, the unusual ideology of the single-firm union, composed of a sense of persecution and a commitment to small enterprise, can hamper the organization. It discourages strategic alliances with other unions, alliances that could boost bargaining strength or provide aid in emergencies. It can be interpreted to discourage affiliation with a multi-union association, despite the contrary advice of union leaders when members misunderstand the ideology's censure of large organizations. It disheartens members by identifying the union with the weaker of two opposing forces, small as opposed to large enterprise. Union members may be aware of the economy-wide drift toward larger organizations, and may be anxious about membership in an isolated, single-shop labor union that elevates smallness to a positive virtue. The ideology and its emotional ties weaken the union by seeming more forceful than they actually are. Unprofessional leaders are not especially skilled at using the ideology; the employer is often anxious to grow larger and has little sentimental devotion to smallness; and recognition of under-dog status can stir demands from the members for improvement of the union's status, possibly even at the cost of losing such other characteristics as plant-orientation and conservative ways.

The personality of the single-firm independent union, or the collective disposition of members and leaders toward principal issues, helps explain the persistence of the organization. The basic personality characteristics, however, have both advantages and disadvantages. Individual unions show modifications of these basic personality characteristics through a wide range. Those which adhere most closely to the characteristics are likely to be weak agents of collective bargaining with contracts

16

Union Personality

that reflect a willingness to accept minimum terms. The unions which most vigorously modify the basic characteristics are strong bargainers with excellent contracts. Weak or strong, however, the single-firm unions still display enough of the characteristics to be easily identified and to mark them off in aims and methods from all other forms of American labor unions.

FOOTNOTES

1. For a study of the "personality" of an organization, see Gellerman, Saul, "The Company's 'Personality,'" *People, Problems and Profits* (New York: McGraw-Hill Book Co., Inc., 1960), pp. 72-93.

2. Part of the explanation for why this study was undertaken when it was involves the availability for the first time in 1960 of extensive public information filed by single-firm unions subject to the reporting requirements of the 1959 Landrum-Griffin Act.

3. Future research might profitably start with a more rigorously selected and more thoroughly representative sample; the sample relied on was the best possible "guess-estimate" under prevailing circumstances. Researchers will soon have available an invaluable aid: Cohany, Harry, "Unaffiliated Local and Single-Employer Unions in the United States," *Monthly Labor Review* (Washington, D.C.: U.S. Department of Labor, Bureau of Labor Statistics, forthcoming).

4. Whenever possible, members were interviewed as well as officers. However, as officers were taken to be representative and also influential primary attention was paid their opinions. Future research might well include shop stewards, rank-and-filers, and possibly even the wives of leaders in a study such as this. For guidance, see Gullahorn, John and Strauss, George, "The Field Worker in Union Research," *Human Organization Research*, Richard N. Adams and Jack J. Preiss, eds. (Homestead, Ill.: The Dorsey Press, Inc., 1960).

5. Re-interviews were used to double-check responses, fill in gaps, and most especially to minimize the effect that a recession may have had on replies first received in 1960.

6. Note that the 40 unions studied were all New Jersey organizations. The highly industrialized character of the state made it a generally representative laboratory for industrial relations research. And the state's large population of single-firm unions (third largest by one government count) afforded ample opportunity to compose what Hughes calls a "process sample": i.e., one that contains a full variety and contrast of different kinds of subject and allows the user to tell the particular from the general. See Hughes, Everett C., "The Sociological Study of Work: An Editorial," *American Journal of Sociology*, LVII (March, 1952), p. 424; Greer, Scott, *Last Man in: Racial Access to Union Power*, (Glencoe, Ill.: The Free Press, 1959), p. 12.

7. Certain topics proved quite revealing. As might be expected, these included such matters as domination, industrial conflict, unions in politics, the merits of size, the importance of power, and others.

III. A COMPARISON OF THE UNION
AND THE LOCAL

THIS comparison of the single-firm independent union with the local of an international union will answer three related questions: How does a local union differ from a single-firm union? What are its advantages and disadvantages in comparison with a local union? How do employers compare the two union types? Answers here shed considerable light on the single-firm union's persistence, its relations with local unions, its history of employer support, and its prospects.

Union Personalities. Judging from the 40 single-firm unions studied in 1960-1961 and from available literature on comparable locals of international unions, the basic personality characteristics of local unions and single-firm unions differ considerably. Although it is "person-based," the local is also responsible to the parent union for extensive record-keeping, adherence to formal procedures, and the use of impersonal communication media such as a local column in the union paper and magazine. Although it is plant-oriented and employer-centered, the local is encouraged by the parent organization to broaden its horizons and it is linked to neighboring locals through strategic alliances and its business agent or international union representative. Although it is conservative in orientation, the local is exposed to the more cosmopolitan thinking and pressure of professional union leaders and staff members. Finally, although it is often as small as most single-firm unions the local generally endorses organizational growth and centralization of authority as right, proper, and "American."[1]

To be sure, the local union and the single-firm independent are similar in many respects. Both are organizations of workers and both have shop-related interests and goals. They are covered by the same labor laws and affected by the same economic climate.[2] Differences, however, overshadow similarities. Unlike the single-firm union, the local union is obliged by its parent international union to incorporate formal as well as informal ways, to look outside as well as inside of the plant, to

18

Comparison with the Local

respond to external liberal as well as internal conservative pressures, and to accept, if not to champion, the growth of the parent union and other favored organizations.

These local union differences from the basic character of the independent union are readily explained by the local's situation. Unlike an independent, the local is not self-contained but rather one of many parts of a much larger organization. The parent body imposes conditions on affiliates designed to augment the effectiveness of the entire organization. Careful record-keeping is a typical condition. There is a high degree of centralization of authority, with central control of revenue and centralized communication media. Local union characteristics reflect obligations and commitments to a parent body. The single-firm union, a self-contained and autonomous organization, is free of such conditions.

Comparative Features. Assuming then, that the local union and the single-firm independent are significantly different organizations, what are the advantages and disadvantages of the independent union in comparison with the local? According to their own leaders, the independent union has at least five important advantages over the local.

Single-firm union members generally pay lower dues than those collected in comparable locals.[3] Moreover, many constitutions expressly forbid assessments for any purpose and thus make a dues increase very difficult to obtain.[4] Independent union leaders linked this "attraction" with that of low overhead. They boasted that members are not taxed to support a full-time union hierarchy or an ambitious union program. While some leaders conceded that low dues meant meager resources and no strike funds, most were convinced the members place a very high value on the unions' low operating costs.

Another advantage of the single-firm union is the limited demands it puts on members. These unions have few committees, activity groups, or delegations to other organizations. Outside of attendance at general membership meetings held as seldom as four times a year, the union member is asked to give very little of his time, energy, or attention. While some leaders feared this leads to apathy and disinterest, most were convinced the members prefer an organization that "doesn't cost them

19

much, gives them damn good service, and doesn't bother them one bit."[5]

The matter of "damn good service" was frequently cited as a major independent union advantage over local unions. Leaders of single-firm independents pointed out that members are in daily contact with officers who have an intimate familiarity with the shop and its problems. There is no interruption in service pending the once-a-month visit or biweekly phone call of a roving business agent as with many local unions. Nor is valuable time lost or mistakes made because "outside" union officials have to be briefed at length. While some officers felt membership reliance on top union officials undermines the shop steward system, most believed on-the-spot, informal, and satisfactory resolution of grievances is a key factor in the single-firm union's persistence.

The internal politics of a single-firm union involves four advantages over those of a local of an international union. Members of independent single-firm unions can "make it from the log cabin to the White House." Within the limits set by standard political processes, a member can hope to attain his union's highest official post.[6] A member knows that at union meetings he has a good chance of being heard and possibly even of influencing others. The number of voters in most single-firm unions is generally small and this enhances the influence of every interested person.[7] Each of the unions is autonomous. It makes all of its decisions and delegates none to higher officials of a parent body.[8] Its accomplishments and its mistakes result from the efforts of co-workers rather than professional administrators, and this contributes to the union's unity and *esprit de corps*. Finally, leaders believe their unions are sure to be free from domination by racketeers or political deviates. All union members are shop employees, and it is argued that no employer will hire or retain lawless or "left-wing" elements.

There were some leaders who recognized that the availability of the union's presidency to all members can result in inferior and transitory leadership. A few felt open discussion and resolution of political questions can impede advisably confidential moves. Some conceded that autonomy often means a lack of sophisticated counsel from outside the organization, and that

Comparison with the Local

the employer may "weed out" unionists he thinks too militant as well as leftists and racketeers. These skeptics are a minority, and even they were impressed by the high regard of the membership for the union's political features.

A final advantage of the single-firm union involves relations with management. Union leaders frequently boasted that amicable union-management relations are due to the union's basic structural and "personality" characteristics: particularly its divorce from other unions, its focus on the plant and the employer, and its open commitment to industrial harmony. These leaders believed local unions are obliged to honor disputes that originated elsewhere among other locals of the parent union. They believed international union representatives stir trouble to justify their salaries or to forward their own political ambitions. And most felt that employers prefer single-firm unions and will help sustain them against local unions.

This, of course, is only half the picture. The union leaders interviewed were neither foolish nor unrealistic. Several, particularly leaders of strong independents, recognized that local unions have advantages over the unaffiliated organizations. Many leaders were willing to concede that local unions offer more services than do single-firm unions. Local unions also bring more bargaining strength into negotiations. Local unions participate sooner and more generously in contract innovations. Local unions benefit from the services of expensive staff experts, and local unions profit from international union influence on the national scene.

These "selling points," once conceded, were quickly qualified by single-firm union supporters who claimed that their members expect and receive services available in local unions from sources outside of the union.[9] Current bargaining strength was thought to be sufficient, and expensive staff advice was thought to be unnecessary if union-management relations were amicable and the employer "appreciated" the union.[10] Contract innovations come the union's way in "due time," and many plant-oriented independent unions do not "give a hang to participate in national politics or other such nonsense."[11]

Employer Perspective. To this point the independent single-firm union and the local union have been compared from the

21

perspective of union leaders and members. Additional insight was offered by 20 businessmen who dealt directly with one or another of the study's 40 single-firm independent unions.[12] Among other things, these men were asked how these unions compare with local unions, and what advantages and shortcomings are involved in dealing with an independent union.

A minority of businessmen felt that single-firm unions and local unions differ little in day-to-day matters.[13] An even smaller number of company representatives complained that the intimate contact of union leaders and members discourages the independent union from policing grievances and hinders its ability to discipline members. Some of these representatives felt the poor educational background of union leaders and the union's lack of staff facilities handicap intelligent discussion of vital economic issues. A few complained that the independent depends too heavily on a single individual, usually a charismatic leader, and is susceptible to great disorder when leadership changes. A small number was distressed by union threats to affiliate unless bargaining demands were met, and one or two were concerned that membership in a multi-union association might lend unwelcomed strength and ideas to the independent union. These businessmen, a decided minority, believed dealings with a local union would not involve the problems mentioned above, though such dealings might entail other equally distressing problems.[14]

The large majority of company representatives scoffed at these complaints. They insisted that the independent's close ties between leader and member and its active grievance machinery constituted a valuable feed-back device for communication purposes. They suggested that educational or staff handicaps could be met with company aid. They felt that turnover problems were common in other labor organizations and presented no special problems. They dismissed union threats to affiliate as bluff tactics, and laughed at the idea that associations would ever make enough of themselves to warrant attention.

The large majority of company representatives was very satisfied with their single-firm independent unions. They particularly valued the ability to make on-the-spot adjustments of

Comparison with the Local

grievances with the highest union officers. They appreciated the intimate familiarity of union officers with shop affairs, and the fact that these officers are career employees with a personal interest in the firm's progress. They lauded the union's commitment to industrial harmony, its reasonableness in negotiations, and its lack of "entangling alliances." Company representatives also valued the union's recognition of "sacred" managerial prerogatives. The union's divorce from political affairs rated high praise as did its lack of reliance on "eggheads," "ivory tower boys," and "leftwing intellectuals."

Some few businessmen also valued the union as a "showpiece" weapon in an ideological struggle against Big Government and Big Unions. These men praised such union features as home-rule and internal democracy, and argued that if only all unions were broken up into single-firm organizations more American workers would enjoy proper union benefits.[15] Whatever the particularly valued feature, the single-firm independent union was generally praised and appreciated by company bargainers—most of whom believed the union offers the company considerably more than available from a local union.[16]

There is more to the difference between the single-firm independent union and the local union than a surface disagreement over optimum union size. The two rivals differ in their basic "personality" as well as in structural features. Reflecting the wishes of members, the single-firm union is generally less formal, less worldly, less progressive, less demanding, and less dynamic than its affiliated counterpart. It also has more in common with employers than do most affiliated locals. The contest between these rivals is by no means one-sided, and this generally unrecognized fact goes far to explain the persistence of the nation's single-firm independent unions.

FOOTNOTES

1. Brooks notes that "union people, by and large, believe nowadays that a union should be big to be effective. . . . This attitude goes be-

Comparison with the Local

yond an argument for the advantages in administrative efficiency and the like. It is a belief that a union of 200,000 members is likely to be twice as good as a union of 100,000 members—twice as good in organizing, in bargaining and in its capacity generally to achieve its primary objectives." Brooks, George W., "Reflections on the Changing Character of American Labor Unions," *Proceedings of the Ninth Annual Meeting* (Madison, Wis.: Industrial Relations Research Association, 1956), p. 37.

2. This similarity between the single-firm union and the local union carries over into the area of union types; there is a weak local as well as a weak single-firm union. For a discussion of weak locals, see Barbash, Jack, *The Practice of Unionism* (New York: Harper, 1956). Note that the pattern of the weak single-firm union is quite similar to one uncovered by Derber, *et al.*, in a recent investigation of local union situations. Derber, Milton, *et al.*, *The Local Union-Management Relationship* (Urbana, Ill.: Institute of Labor and Industrial Relations, University of Illinois, 1960), pp. 62, 67.

3. Of 39,650 local unions reporting to the Federal Government in 1960, 7,955 locals had a prevailing dues fee of less than $3 (or 20 per cent of the sample). *A Report of the Bureau of Labor-Management Reports: Fiscal Year, 1960* (Washington, D.C.: Bureau of Labor Statistics, Bulletin 1265-28), p. 26. Of 40 single-firm unions studied in 1960-1961, 30 unions collected dues of less than $3 (or 75 per cent of the sample). Single-firm union leaders make much of this difference. Weber's analysis of the situation in the chemical industry points up the real price advantage enjoyed by the independents over the international unions: "Adherents of independent unionism have long used the per capita tax as a convenient symbol of the 'outside' exploitation which could be expected in the event that the rank and file ever voted for affiliation." Weber, Arnold, R., "Competitive Unionism in the Chemical Industry," *Industrial and Labor Relations Review*, 13 (October, 1959), p. 24.

4. Over half the local unions reporting in 1960 charged an initiation fee of more than $5 and a tenth of them charged $100 or more. Less than one-third of the single firm independent unions studied charged fees of more than $5 and none charged more than $10. *A Report . . . , op. cit.,* p. 28.

5. "Leave-me-alone-unionism" has no necessary connection with substandard unionism. Brooks contends that "to regard attendance at union meetings as some kind of index of the health of a union is very far from the mark." Kovner and Lahne argue that "the 'shop society' or informal communications inside and outside of the plant are more significant than union meetings. . . . It is very difficult to see why or how a local union would be better off if most of its members attended all of its meetings." Brooks, George W., *The Sources of Vitality in the American Labor Movement* (Ithaca, N.Y.: N.Y. School of Industrial and Labor Relations, Bulletin No. 41, 1960), pp. 5, 7. See also Kovner, Joseph, and Lahne, Herbert J., "Shop Society and the Unions," *Industrial and Labor Relations Review*, 7 (October, 1953), pp. 4-24.

6. While political advance is theoretically possible in international unions, research suggests members feel they do not have adequate educational backgrounds and they "have strong doubts about their resoluteness in talking back to management." Barbash, Jack, *Labor's Grass Roots* (New York: Harper, 1961), p. 211. In contrast, single-firm union mem-

Comparison with the Local

bers and leaders have comparable educational backgrounds (all are shop members) and these unions more often talk with rather than back to management.

7. In a related context Kerr suggests that: "In the one-plant local, rival leaders can get known and be effective, issues can be discussed on a face-to-face basis, and democracy can be effective. . . . The multiplant unit serves the interests of the entrenched leadership in a most emphatic way. The one-plant local with real authority is the most democratic entity in the trade-union movement." Kerr, Clark, "Unions and Union Leaders of Their Own Choosing," *The Next Twenty Years in Industrial Relations* (Cambridge, Mass.: Industrial Relations Section, MIT, 1957), p. 61. Weber suggests that the single-firm unions are not always exemplars of internal democracy. ". . . In the absence of any external checks, autonomy has sometimes served as a cloak for questionable internal practices." Weber, Arnold R., "Competitive Unionism in the Chemical Industry," *op. cit.*, p. 33.

8. Brooks maintains that the delegation of decision-making in certain international unions has gone so far as to deprive the local of any meaningful role. Brooks, *The Sources of Vitality in the American Labor Movement, op. cit.*, p. 7. Dalton notes considerable resentment by local union (and management) personnel against outplant interference with local autonomy. Dalton, Melville, *Men Who Manage* (New York: John Wiley and Sons, Inc., 1959), p. 111.

9. Independent union leaders claim such local union services as adult education programs, vacation tours, discount shops, and others are best left a private matter for the worker himself. They also maintain that non-union sources are plentiful and that scarce union resources should not be earmarked for such non-essentials.

10. Brooks points out that: "The essential relationship in an *established* collective bargaining relationship is the relationship between the union leadership and the industrial relations office. This is not a 'power' relationship, but an accommodation to each other, and except in rare instances the use of the word 'power' is not only incorrect, it is irrelevant." Brooks, *The Sources of Vitality in the American Labor Movement, op. cit.*, p. 22. Independent unions fear that staff officials cannot be controlled and this fear helps minimize jealousy of the staff facilities of comparable local unions.

11. For evidence of competitiveness in contract terms, see Chapter 5, "The Blue-Collar Union As A Strong Union." Weber attributes much of the single-firm union's success in the chemical industry to "relatively high wage levels and generous fringe benefits." Weber, Arnold, *op. cit.* Purcell finds that contracts of single-firm independents in the meatpacking industry differ little from contracts of two comparable local unions. Purcell, Theodore V., S. J., *Blue Collar Man* (Cambridge, Mass.: Harvard University Press, 1960); p. 27. Marshall's study of an independent at the largest refinery in the United States established that contract terms were better than those of other nearby unions. Marshall, F. Ray, "Independent Unions in the Gulf Coast Petroleum Refining Industry—The Esso Experience," *Labor Law Journal*, September, 1961, pp. 823-840. Troy concludes that in the telephone industry the single-firm union's "terms of employment are usually as good as or better than those of comparable

25

Comparison with the Local

affiliated unions." Troy, "Local Independent and National Unions: Competitive Labor Organizations," *Journal of Political Economy*, LXVIII (October, 1960), p. 494. See also Walton, Richard E., *The Impact of the Professional Engineering Union* (Boston, Mass.: Harvard University, 1961).

12. See also "The Case for the Local Independent Union," *Personnel*, 32 (November, 1955), pp. 226-234; Weber, Arnold, *op. cit.*; Marshall, F. Ray, *op. cit.*, pp. 824, 840. The writer's sample unfortunately does not include any first-line supervisors or more than one company president. (Most of the respondents were industrial relations or personnel specialists.) The sample is small, the interviews were conducted a year after the union representatives were seen, and the respondents were very cautious. Future research is definitely called for; definitive findings wait on a larger sample—and less cautious respondents.

13. The few company representatives who equate independents and locals are older, more experienced men who have come "up the line" from the shop. These men have dealt with more and varied unions than have the other respondents.

14. The company representatives who would prefer to deal with a local union are usually involved in antagonistic or arms-length relations with a strong independent. Marshall notes that employers "apparently view independent unions with mixed emotions. . . . A major difficulty has been that independents do not always know what is possible in collective bargaining. They are sometimes not satisfied even when they get a good contract because they don't always know what is possible." Marshall, F. Ray, *op. cit.*, p. 840.

15. Staff-based younger company representatives are particular admirers of the single-firm independent union; they recognize and applaud the close congruity between the union and their own ideological preference for a narrow, restricted trade union. With these men the union becomes something more than the freely-chosen employee representative the law requires them to deal with. It is also embraced as a symbol of the desirable way of things.

16. For indirect evidence that at least some employers are still attracted by the weak union's susceptibility to the rewards of paternalism, see Selekman, Benjamin M., *A Moral Philosophy for Management* (New York: McGraw-Hill Book Co., 1959); Magoun, F. Alexander, *Cooperation and Conflict in Industry* (New York: Harper & Brothers, 1960); Spates, Thomas G., *Human Values Where People Work* (New York: Harper & Brothers, 1960); Blum, Albert A., "Personal Policy and the Worker," *IUD Digest*, Winter 1961, pp. 120-128. See also annual reports of cases handled by the NLRB involving employer domination of both local unions and single-firm unaffiliated organizations.

IV. THE BLUE-COLLAR UNION
AS A WEAK UNION

SINGLE-FIRM independent unions of blue-collar workers are the oldest, most numerous, most popular, and most threatened of all such unions. They are older than similar unions of white-collar workers by thirty or more years. They outnumber unions of white-collar workers in total and membership figures. They face the most powerful and aggressive of international unions.

It was possible to divide the study's 36 blue-collar unions along many dimensions. The old could be separated from the young, the large from the small, the factory union from the union in a service enterprise, and so forth. A careful consideration of such dimensions suggested one that incorporated the others and advanced analysis farther than any other single one. This dimension focuses on *strength in collective bargaining*. Such strength was found to be the best single index to a variety of related union characteristics. For example, the stronger the bargainer, the greater the likelihood that it is led by talented, vigorous, young men, that it is large in size, and that it has interests outside the shop. Of course, the unions range the full gamut on a continuum of bargaining strength. It is fair and useful, however, to center discussion about polar types, the weak and the strong bargainer.[1]

The weak single-firm union is one which pursues the goal of accepting ends set for it by an employer. It does not maintain a balance of power in negotiations. While it formally has a decision-making mechanism of its own, in practice this mechanism is in the service of the employer. The weak bargainer is theoretically free to reject contract terms "suggested" in negotiations, but, in fact, its power is very limited and it has no "taste" for conflict.[2]

A weak bargainer manifests some combination of these characteristics:

1) It makes few preparations for negotiations, settles a contract in an afternoon, and accepts a contract that

compares poorly with prevailing area and industry terms.

2) It allows members to circumvent the grievance machinery and avoids the threat of militant acts to promote greater contract gains.

3) It consents to the employer's division of authority in shop matters and welcomes the rewards of paternalism.[3]

Special circumstances of the weak bargainers help explain such a performance. In general they are relatively new small unions, in rural locations, organized on the basis of opposition to big international unions. Their leaders are generally older men. The consequences of each circumstance are examined below.

Weak independent unions are not descendants of company unions of the 1930's. While some such survivors persist in the protective isolation of rural or very small shops, most of the weak unions surveyed had been formed in the last ten years. This youthfulness means lack of experience, precedents, guides, and often even a lack of standards. The union is led by neophytes whose inadequacies are compounded by their inability to devote full time to the union and by the union's isolation from other labor organizations.

The weak independent union is small. Most of the unions studied had less than one hundred members. This sets a limit on union resources from the very start—particularly when the union restricts its potential resources to those of a single employer's employees. Small size also encourages a close-knit work community, with the employer in a small shop frequently enjoying a warm first-name relationship with his employees.[4] These employees are usually senior, highly committed personnel of considerable value to the company. Work conditions are generally tolerable if only because the technology is stable as the employer cannot afford extensive modernization, and the workers are accustomed to the shop.[5] Supervisors are few and are usually drawn from the ranks. There is, in short, a close, if often one-sided relationship between labor and management.

Typical of the small shops that support weak single-firm unions was one described by its leader in these words:

Weak Unions

"We are a standby coke conversion plant. The company doesn't pay us any mind anymore since it no longer makes gas out of coke. The group here has come down from five hundred to eighty. Half of the men left have 25 years seniority or more, and the average man in the plant is 55 years old. We are dying off, and when we are almost all gone, they'll probably close the damn place altogether. We tell them to keep a spare tire for trips across the desert, but they are no longer buying this argument."*

The president of a weak union in an animal feed mill reported that:

"We are only 19 men. Most have five or six years' seniority and the average man is about 45 years old. I don't know why we ever did bother to unionize; we have no need for it. We don't have any arguments with the mill owners. Why, we are just like one big family."

A third single-firm independent union included all 16 employees of a small lumberyard. Its leader characteristically reported that the members got "nothing from this union but protection from the Teamsters."

Most weak bargainers are formed to escape the organizing efforts of an international union.[6] The international union may be judged undesirable by either the employer, his employees, or both. They are frightened by the international union's actual or presumed use of violence and the actual or presumed presence of racketeers, "leftists," or "dictators." They also oppose the high dues, centralized authority, assessments, sympathy strikes, political activities and high executive salaries of the internationals.[7]

A typical weak union in the sample had been formed in 1958 in opposition to the aggressive organizing tactics of the International Teamsters Union. The 16 lumberyard workers involved had been thoroughly frightened and antagonized when their spokesman received threatening phone calls late at night, had paint splattered on his home and car, found nails strewn

---

* This quotation and subsequent quotations which are not attributed by name are from privileged communications with the author.

in his driveway and was eventually forced to request police protection. The lumberyard employees pledged then to avoid the Teamsters at any cost, even when that meant the formation of a weak, passive union.

In a similar case, the president of a weak union of 35 sweater makers recalled that:

> "The ILGWU started to visit us at our homes in 1959. They were polite, and tried persuasion. No threats, you understand. But later they wanted to keep us from working so they could force the boss to sign a contract. They punched a presser in the nose when he tried to come into the shop and they phoned in a bomb scare. The girls got pretty frightened. . . . I never liked the IL because it forced me out of the business a few years ago when a little shop I owned couldn't give a pay raise. So I decided to form an independent union and I called a lawyer . . . by this time the girls were ready to come along for the ride."

Few shops studied had as poor a contract as did this one. The terms were settled by "opposing" lawyers, while the parties sat in silence.

A union organized on the basis of rejection of the big unions faces two debilitating problems: self-imposed isolation from the main stream of the American labor movement, and the pressure to win immediate gains from the employer. An employer interested in such a weak union can trade immediate contract gains for an "understanding" regarding the long-term division of authority in the shop.

These weak independent unions have semi-rural or urban fringe locations. This contributes to their plight in several ways. For one, valuable services that unions need are not always available. The president of a rural union of 65 lumber mill workers noted:

> "One of our big problems is that there are no labor lawyers in the area. We tried to use two local men but they knew little of the labor law and were too friendly with the boss. The mill owners are aware of this and take advantage

by offering to let us see the books at bargaining time. They know we are too ignorant to understand the figures. We have sent upstate for a good lawyer but we don't have the money to bring him here often enough. It's tough when you try to run a union out in the sticks."

Another problem is that employers often enjoy more prestige and influence in semi-rural areas than their counterparts do in urban centers. These single-firm unions are not immediately exposed to comparison with more powerful and resourceful locals of international unions. The atmosphere in semi-rural locations encourages a very limited union by discouraging certain union functions such as the strike and certain union services such as participation in local government.[8]

Weak bargainers are generally led by older workers of long seniority. These men take pride in warm friendships with the people in management. Half of the presidents of weak unions interviewed were older than 55 years.[9] One such president, a gentleman of 67 years, carefully explained:

"Most unions overdo it. They push the company too far. Mind, I am 100 per cent for unions. In my own situation, however, I go 52 per cent for the company and 48 per cent for my union. I make it a point to jump on shirkers before the company sees them. That way, there is no trouble. Never no cussing; all is reasoned out on a friendly basis. So I can't see nothing wrong with my union."

Older leaders, like this man, hope to retire soon from their present jobs and place a high value on their accrued retirement benefits. Anything which threatens the continued prosperity of their employer, such as unsettled labor relations, threatens the satisfactory completion of their worklives. Such men represent the viewpoint of maximum commitment to industrial harmony.

Moreover, these men are eager for promotion as faithful compliant employees. Many leaders of weak unions hoped the employer would someday offer them positions as foremen; and, given their considerable seniority, several leaders felt the offer was imminent. This possibility of promotion into the ranks of

Weak Unions

management conditions the behavior and attitudes of weak union leaders. One of these men suggested as much in an unusually candid comment:

> "Since 1943 when we organized this union, I've been meeting and going around with other [independent] union leaders. Take my word for it, 98 per cent of the top men of independent unions are very easily bought, not with money, but with promotions. To be any good in this job, you have to forget yourself. These other guys never forget the big 'me,' but find it easy to forget the union when promotion time comes. Hell, 12 of 30 bosses in this place alone are former officers in my union."

Few other leaders were as blunt—or as critical of the practice.

It was not surprising, accordingly, to learn that the leaders of weak unions have a conservative conception of trade unionism, one that faithfully reflects their plant-orientation. Nine of ten leaders interviewed believed labor unions should not participate in politics and should certainly not use union funds for political purposes. None of the unions they led endorsed candidates for political office and only two of them participated indirectly in politics through membership in a state or national multi-union association. The majority of the leaders approved of right-to-work (anti-union-shop) laws even though almost all had a union shop clause in their contracts, often inserted by employers anxious to preserve the union. The majority also believed that organized labor constitutes a monopoly threat to the economy and is even more corrupt than suggested by the McClellan Committee.

It is plain that many of the weak union leaders did not fully understand the subjects about which they expressed predominantly conservative opinions. For example, the 61-year old leader of a union of 16 lumber yard employees reported:

> "I believe in the right-to-work laws. A man should be able to work without a union getting in his way. No, I don't see any contradiction between this position and the union-shop clause in our contract. But mind, I am sure against what you fellows call 'free riders.'"

Weak Unions

Another leader noted that:

"... the ILGWU wanted me to join their staff as an organizer. They really admired the job I did in organizing my own union. I said 'No,' that line of work is plain racketeering. And no wonder, what with racketeers like Reuther and Meany and Hoffa heading up the big unions. Under these guys the big unions make excessive demands and close up shops. I don't want any part of it."

Very few of the leaders of weak unions knew how many unionists there are in the country or approximately how many international unions exist. Lack of these and related facts, however, did not hamper the expression of deeply-felt and highly persuasive criticisms of international trade unionism.

Simplicity is the prime characteristic of the weak union's services. Given their disinterest in traditional union ways, the leaders of such weak unions are fortunate in having few union tasks to perform. In the matter of services, the weak bargainer offers nothing to compare with big union features such as picnics, dances, ceremonial dinners, discount tickets, access to resort or retirement centers, job advancement courses, union career training, hobby clubs, and others. The services of the weak union are limited in most cases to free legal counsel, a service standard elsewhere in the labor movement.[10]

A typical weak union, one composed of 86 oil depot drivers and helpers, had a common service record. Its leader recalled that:

"... we used to charge 25 cents dues a member a month. But nobody was really interested so we had no money in the treasury from the start in 1938 up until the present. We ran a few dances in '38 and '39 but nothing like that since. Now, however, we hope to get something going. The McClellan Committee stuff got the boys interested in our union again, they don't want no Teamsters in here. So we bought a coke machine and make some money in that way. We also raised dues a little and, more importantly, we have begun to collect dues. We can afford candy for guys in the hospital and a funeral piece if that becomes necessary. There is a new life in our organization. No telling, as more old men die and younger fellows take an interest our union may really begin to offer something."

Another weak union was heading in the opposite direction:

"Our dues now are $3 a member a month. With 47 men paying, we throw a Christmas party for our kids that costs $175 and meet installments on our $7,000 legal bill [incurred fighting a raid for two years]. The men don't complain about the three dollars; our dairy routes are good ones. But I want to reduce the dues anyhow. Once the lawyers are paid we will go down to $1 a member a month. Too much money can lead to greediness or beer parties. I don't want to put temptation in front of the men. We only need $20 rent annually for a meeting place and a few dollars for a secretary. No need for the union to offer anything else, except maybe the Christmas party."

This last was a representative opinion of leaders of weak unions.

The weak union's labor-management relations could not be simpler. To begin with, such a union makes no attempt to gather data, compare contracts, or in any other way prepare for negotiations. The union leader of 86 oil depot workers offered a typical report:

"We don't bother to prepare. Our drivers learn things from other drivers and this is usually enough. . . . Of course, we don't pick up anything but what the company has first offered it, but we can't complain. . . ."

Another man, the president of a 95-man union in a battery manufacturing company related that:

"The committee members talk about what we want among ourselves for about a week before negotiations. Then we go up to the vice-president's office and he reads us the contracts negotiated by the internationals in the company's other plants. We nod our heads if we agree or chew it over if we don't. We usually agree."

Weak Unions

The weak union does not employ such standard negotiation tools as a mass meeting to resolve demands, a ceremonial strike vote, or a token assessment for a strike fund. It does not use specific data in negotiations, trusting the partial knowledge of union officers and the self-serving data of management.[11] Negotiations are informal, friendly and swift.

To their credit, the union leaders interviewed did not overestimate the results. Most declined to evaluate their contracts; a few judged them average in the area and for the industry. A comparison of the contract terms of weak unaffiliated unions with data compiled by the Bureau of Labor Statistics confirms the modest appraisal.[12] At the same time, however, it suggests that employers do not allow these unions to fall too far behind competitive labor standards. It also suggests that outside agents such as a governmental price-fixing board, or an employers' association, or the local of an international union at a sister plant can and do help such weak unions win respectable contract terms, regardless of the union's strength.

For example, in the dairy industry the State Milk Board, an outside agent, indirectly determines labor contract conditions through its price-setting mechanism. The leader of 47 milk truck drivers shrugged his shoulders when asked if his union required more bargaining strength:

> "What the hell, the Milk Board writes our contract. Not even the boss has any say. The Board tells us what we can charge for our product and the boss gives us a fair portion of that. He levels with us and we wait on the Board."

Interestingly, not all the employees of this dairy agreed with the president. After the independent union was organized the employer fired four senior workers who had favored bringing in a strong international union.

Some employers are not as willing to preserve the union's position in the shop as they are to provide competitive contract terms. The weak independent union is distinguished for its lack of influence in shop matters. Such crucial items as the level of work performance, promotion to nonsupervisory positions, and job content are considered beyond the union's

Weak Unions

proper range.[13] For example, none of the union leaders interviewed met regularly with management to discuss plant problems and none bothered to record infrequent grievances. Naturally none of these weak unions had ever taken a case to arbitration or conducted a strike.

In keeping with this record of mutual trust (or one-sided relations), these aging conservative union leaders expressed considerable faith in their employers. Most of them rejected the notion that management abuses its power or undermines the union through direct dealings with the employees. (In these weak unions an employee could bypass the grievance machinery and go directly to the employer.) Almost all of the union leaders believed top management was reasonable and efficient. The company was also credited with understanding the personal problems of the union president.

This faith in the employer was succinctly expressed by the leader of a weak union of 35 sweater makers who replied, when asked what data he used in negotiations, that:

> "I don't use any stuff. We have no idea of how the company is doing, except we believe the boss when he tells us business stinks. We can see it by looking around the shop; we trust the employer. . . ."

This same leader reported his union's biggest problem was worker jealousy over wage differences.

> "All the girls want equalization. So I take the individual grievances to the boss. I generally always agree with his reasons for turning down the request for more. . . ."

Another union president recalled that when his shop was first being organized by proponents of a big union he went to the employer:

> ". . . and I offered to watch the guys and bring him back news of their plans. I liked the Old Man a good deal and would do a lot to help him. He was surprised and upset about the men. . . . After he fired the key six he asked me what to do. I suggested he let me form an independent union. The Old Man liked the idea and has been fair and honest with my union ever since. . . . In the shop, no mat-

36

ter what the subject, we leave it all up to the Old Man. His judgment is far superior to ours."

While most leaders of weak unions do not go as far as the man above in demonstrating their admiration for and faith in the employer, they share these sentiments with very few reservations.

This trust in the employer is encouraged by a calculated program of company paternalism. In addition to lending a helping hand during the union's formation and during negotiations, many employers sponsor holiday shop parties, lend money to employees, forgive garnishees, help support employee bowling and softball teams, and in other similar ways demonstrate their concern with employees. Employers explained such support in two ways: it helps "keep out the Teamsters" or some other international union the employer fears, and it acknowledges positive contributions by the existing union. These include the union's narrow focus on the shop, its commitment to industrial harmony, its single-plant location, and the trusting nature of its leaders. Some employers also advanced an ideological explanation. They value the weak union's lack of interest in politics, its distance from other unions, its freedom from left-wing or racketeer domination, and its lack of extra-economic functions such as educational, social, or recreational activities.

The tasks of union government are minimized by the weak program. Employer support of weak single-firm unions and provision of services further reduces the tasks of union government. The task, for example, of administering union dollars is made easy by the weak bargainers' lack of funds. They collect token dues and never levy assessments. Almost all of the unions studied collected two dollars or less per member; one union managed on 25 cents dues. The president explained:

> "We just don't have any expenses. I've got 95 men paying monthly so we collect close to three hundred bucks a year. We pay $20 rent annually for a meeting hall, spend $15 for an occasional retirement gift, buy the widow a $10 flower piece if one of the boys dies, and help the boss throw a little Christmas party in the shop. . . . What else is there for a union to do with its money?"

Weak Unions

Other leaders of weak single-firm unions added that a low dues structure helped keep members wary of the three and four dollar dues schedule of most international unions.[14]

Meetings are as simple a matter as the administration of small treasuries. The meetings are few in number; the attendance is large; and the program is brief. The "large" attendance can be explained by the close-knit nature of small work groups, the use of company property and the lunch hour for meetings, or the offer of a free beer-and-sandwich spread. Leaders of weak unions also cited negative "encouragements" in explaining attendance. These include fines, the threat of expulsion, social harassment, and the possibility that members would ostracize the absentees.[15] Despite their characterization of attendance as "large" and the presence of inducements and penalties, almost all of these weak union presidents complained that attendance, interest, and meeting participation could and should be improved. Few, however, had any concrete plans for doing so.

A cardinal meeting event, the election of officers, is probably typical of all business in these unions. The elections were reportedly calm, colorless, and contrived. A few old cronies circulated the posts or an incumbent consented to another term because "no one else would take the damn job." This is not surprising since the job has no material rewards such as superseniority, a salary, or lost-time expenses and has only the prestige owed a powerless position. This is not to suggest, however, that the leaders of these weak single-firm unions are without standard union problems such as dissension over a craft differential or standard single-firm union problems such as lack of funds. This is to suggest that union weakness, in frequent combination with employer paternalism, effectively reduces the content, and attractiveness, of the president's post.

The weak single-firm independent union is supported by a whole set of circumstances which make its weakness as the representative of its members a paradoxical advantage to it. In

Weak Unions

effect the members of these unions reject the contemporary idea of the functions of a labor union, and they specifically reject being identified as "labor" themselves. The prime usefulness of their unions to them is the protection they offer from organization by the international unions. These members, older men with the conservative attitudes of rural America, do not want their interests guarded by a militant union; they prefer to show their confidence in their employers' benevolence. They are not eager for legislation to protect the rights of workers and their unions; they do not want the involvement and responsibility of membership in a powerful labor organization. Their unions, weak bargainers, undemanding of them or of their employers, are the expression of these feelings.

FOOTNOTES

1. Weak and strong single-firm unions were distinguished by their preparations for, conduct in, and results of negotiations, as well as the union's militancy, and the degree of employer paternalism.

2. Although labor legislation explicitly prohibits employer-domination of unions, the weak single-firm unions persist in spite of the law. For one thing, as a result of Wagner Act prohibitions, the weak unions are influenced, rather than dominated. The methods of control are difficult to demonstrate in an NLRB hearing, and many are legal, if ethically suspect. The employer is also protected both by the NLRB's inability to produce the type of evidence demanded by the courts and by the fact that 39 states have no prohibition against employer domination of local labor organizations. The eleven states with prohibitions include Colorado, Connecticut, Hawaii, Kansas, Massachusetts, Michigan, New York, Pennsylvania, Rhode Island, Utah, and Wisconsin. For details, see U.S. Department of Labor, *State Labor Relations Act* (Washington, D.C.: Bureau of Labor Standards, Bulletin 224, January, 1961), pp. 12, 14. It is revealing that only one of the states (New York) publishes a directory that lists intra-state single-firm unions.

3. Unfortunately, it is not yet possible to estimate how many single-firm unions are weak unions. Half of the writer's sample of 36 blue-collar unions were weak unions; well over half of all the single-firm unions described in the literature appear to be weak unions.

4. "One of the major advantages of small size is the plant atmosphere it provides. . . . Small plant size allows the intimate contact necessary to know one's workers and to provide them with a large variety of personal services, both of which contribute to good industrial relations." Cleland, Sherrill, *The Influence of Plant Size on Industrial Relations* (Princeton, N.J.: Industrial Relations Section, Princeton University, 1955), p. 62.

5. New evidence suggests that technology goes a long way toward explaining why a union in one shop is weak while a similar union in a dissimilar shop is strong. Sayles points out that "the human element, so-called, is a resultant of the technological decisions and, in part at least, predictable from them." Sayles, Leonard, *Behavior of Industrial Work Groups* (New York: John Wiley & Sons, Inc., 1958), p. 5. Blauner focuses on continuous-flow industries and concludes that the technology encourages "a middle-class psychology, a long-range time perspective, planning for one's personal future and for long-term career with the same employer." These ingredients help explain the presence of the single-firm union in such continuous-flow industries as chemicals and petroleum. Blauner, Robert, "Work Satisfaction and Industrial Trends in Modern Society," *Labor and Trade Unionism*, Walter Galenson and Seymour Martin Lipset, eds. (New York: John Wiley & Sons, Inc., 1960), pp. 339-360.

6. My research suggests the major reason for formation has changed considerably over the last thirty years. In the decade 1930-1940, the reason was employer's instigation; in the decade 1940-1950, unrest traceable to wartime production conditions; and from about 1950 to the present, the major reason for formation has been opposition to a major union, opposition often shared by the employees with their employer. Almost all of the weak unions originate in this period.

7. The reasons for electing a weak union have not changed for the last thirty or more years. See, for example, American Iron and Steel Institute, *Employee Representation in the Iron and Steel Industry*. (New York: American Iron and Steel Institute, 1935); Millis, Harry A., and Montgomery, Royal E., *The Economics of Labor* (New York: McGraw-Hill Book Co., Inc., 1945), p. 873.

8. For discussion of local parochialism antithetical to standard trade unionism, see Seidman, Joel, *et al.*, *The Worker Views His Union* (Chicago, Ill.: University of Chicago Press, 1958), pp. 116-117; 124-125; Karsh, Bernard, *Diary of a Strike* (Urbana, Ill.: University of Illinois Press, 1958). On the lesser interest in unions of workers with a rural rather than an urban background, see Tagliacozzo, Daisy and Seidman, Joel, "A Typology of Rank and File Union Members," *American Journal of Sociology*, LI (May, 1956), p. 548; Form, William H. and Dansereau, H. K., "Union Member Orientations and Patterns of Social Integration," *Industrial and Labor Relations Review*, 11 (October, 1957), p. 10; Kornhauser, Ruth, "Some Social Determinants and Consequences of Union Membership," *Labor History* (Winter 1961), pp. 53-54. Note that the only state directory that distinguishes between city and outlying location of single-firm unions reveals that in four of seven areas more single-firm unions are located in the outlying region. New York State Department of Labor, *Directory of Labor Organizations in New York State* (New York: Division of Research and Statistics, Bulletin 233, 1959).

9. Data indicates that unions in small plants (less than 500 employees) are generally led by older, skilled workers who appear more conservative, less militant, and better able to see management's point of view than the leaders of large locals. Cleland, Sherrill, *op. cit.*, p. 14. On the job-related attitudes of older workers, see Herzberg, Frederick, *et al.*, *Job Attitudes* (Pittsburgh, Pa.: Psychological Service of Pittsburgh, 1957);

Weak Unions

Palmer, Gladys L., "Attitudes Toward Work in an Industrial Community," *American Journal of Sociology*, LIII (July, 1957), pp. 17-26.

10. Some lawyers reportedly use "free advice" to create unethically expensive business for themselves. This practice is less common in international unions where attorneys are salaried staff members. It is also revealing that a recently proposed code of ethics for personnel directors labelled as improper "paying a lawyer to act for an independent union." Anonymous, "Ethics in Personnel Administration," *Personnel*, November 1953, p. 185.

11. The weak single-firm union depends heavily in bargaining on the knowledge that employee-members have of the employer's business record. Pertinent studies suggest this is an unreliable source of data; exaggeration and incomplete knowledge frequently mar reports from employees. See Keown, William H., *Some Dimensions of Company-Union Downward Communication* (Madison, Wisconsin: Bureau of Business Research and Service, School of Commerce, University of Wisconsin, 1955); Perry, Dallis and Mahoney, Thomas A., "In-Plant Communication and Employee Morale," *Personnel Psychology*, 8 (1955), pp. 339-346; Fagg, Donald R., *et al.*, "What the Factory Worker Knows about His Factory," *Journal of Business*, 31 (July, 1958), pp. 213-235; Hardin, Einar and Hershey, Gerald L., "Accuracy of Employee Reports on Changes in Pay," *Journal of Applied Psychology*, 44 (1960), pp. 269-275.

12. Contract terms of weak single-firm unions were compared with terms in U.S. Department of Labor, *Occupational Wage Survey: Newark and Jersey City: February 1960* (Washington, D.C.: Bureau of Labor Statistics, Bulletin No. 1265-28). Allowance was made for the fact that the units surveyed by the BLS were large and were located in large urban areas. Note that a company willing or compelled to grant competitive contract terms still has ample reason in day-to-day shop affairs to value its influence over a weak union and prefers this union to alternatives.

13. Limited influence in shop affairs is also common to small locals of international unions. However, the difference between limited influence with and without backup resources is a difference in kind rather than degree.

14. Data on international unions are available in U.S. Department of Labor, *A Report of the Bureau of Labor-Management Reports: Fiscal Year, 1960* (Washington, D.C.: Bureau of Labor-Management Reports, 1960), p. 26.

15. A note of caution is in order as the claim of high attendance was not verified by direct observation. Some exaggeration is likely since union leaders often consider high attendance a personal compliment. On fraud in such reporting, see Dean, Lois, "Interaction, Reported and Observed: The Case of One Local Union," *Human Organization*, XVII (Fall, 1958), pp. 36-44. For support of the notion that small organizations frequently enjoy high meeting attendance, see Spinrad, William, *op. cit.*, pp. 237-245.

V. THE BLUE-COLLAR UNION
AS A STRONG UNION

WHILE many independent unions can be found crowding the "weak" end of a continuum measuring strength in collective bargaining, many others are found at the opposite "strong" pole. These able unions are generally in excellent "fighting trim." They take an assertive approach to their labor-management relations and operate with a relatively complex structure. Specifically, the unions identified as strong unions for this study were those which advance and pursue goals of their own making. They maintain a balance of power and have an independent decision-making mechanism. They prepare carefully for bargaining, bargain strenuously and are not afraid to strike if necessary. In almost every way the strong union differs from the weak single-firm independent union.[1]

The strong union dates back many years. A third of the eighteen strong organizations studied had been formed in the 1930's, a third in the 1940's, and a third in the 1950's. This distribution suggests that most strong blue-collar bargainers have had many years to free themselves from early domination or to consolidate early strength.

These strong unions have a variety of origins. Half of those studied had a history of employer domination and had been formed as employer buffers against international unions. The other half had been formed either after an unsuccessful strike by a big union local it then replaced, or as a result of craft worker dissatisfaction with a craft differential, or simply as a consequence of widespread employee discontent. The heat of these early struggles forged an independent, often distrustful spirit and a recognition of the need for a strong union.[2]

The president of a strong independent union of 2,000 toilet goods company employees offered a characteristic story of union change and development:

> "Our union was formed back in 1935. The company was behind the move because the CIO boys were sniffing around. The city's mayor also played a hand. He promised local companies that he would bar the CIO from the area

42

Strong Unions

and favor the AFL building trade outfits. The Wagner Act
fixed him but our union remained company-dominated
until 1940. That year the Company turned down our demand for paid holidays and we pulled off a quickie strike
as a demonstration. At the next union election the members voted in a whole new slate. They figured if we were
going to have to strike they wanted militant and not spine-
less leadership. We started on the road to independence. . . ."

Another leader, who headed a union of 450 filter company
employees, recalled:

"We got started around 1941. The company grew too
quickly with war work and the new foremen they put on
were too rough on us. So we organized. The president of
the company called us in and said he was shocked. He
made a lot of promises to make us change our minds, but
when they were broken we moved again. The AFL got
wind of the drive and forced an election. We got the company's endorsement without seeking it and that was worth
a few votes, but we felt from the start that the broken
promises cleared us of any debt to the company."

The leader of a strong single-firm union of an insulation manu-
facturer told this tale:

"When the company opened this branch a few years ago
it had two employees. The AFL union that it bargained
with for 37 years at the Minnesota plant signed a new
sweetheart agreement covering these two employees. Then
the company began to grow and soon the plant had over
170 workers. When we learned the contract had been
written in Minnesota in 1928 and hardly improved since,
we called a wildcat strike. After 30 days the company and
the AFL agreed to an election. My independent union
won by 168 to 3. The company was fit to be tied and refused to cooperate. So we struck again for 63 days. We've
been out for 93 days in the last two years, and I think
we're going to strike again in April. We're going to get a
modern contract, or know why."

Strong Unions

Other leaders of strong independents told similar stories of early opposition to their unions and the consequent strengthening of the commitment of members.

The strong union shows a wide range in size. A third of those studied had less than 100 members (as did all weak unions studied): nine had between 100 and 500 members, and the others had 650, 1,700, and 2,200 members. These numbers reflect members available for committee service and even for picket duty. The numbers represent a source of strength not available to the relatively small, weak unions. Similarly, the industrial distribution of the strong unions implies a type of reinforcement denied the weak unions. The strong unions are concentrated in subsidiaries of large corporations rather than in small, locally-owned shops. This means they have the protection of Federal prohibitions against domination. (The Wagner Act ban applies only in interstate commerce.) They deal with relatively sophisticated managements and they can occasionally by-pass local plant managers in favor of profitable deals with headquarters officials.[3]

The strong unions are mostly located in urban industrial centers. This is probably due to the large manpower requirements of the employers and to the fact that most of the plants involved were built before the current interest in industrial dispersion. An urban location encourages union strength because it means the union is in imminent danger of a raid from internationals and it is exposed at first-hand to their standards of active participation in city government, in charity drives and in health and welfare organizations. To judge from the many services strong unions were seen to offer, exposure generally encourages the expansion of the role of the independent single-firm union.

The leaders of strong bargainers are usually middle-aged men of great personal dynamism. This quality distinguishes between strong and weak unions more effectively than any other. The presidents of the strong unions studied ranged in age from 34 to 60 years; the average president was 42 years old, seven years younger than his counterpart in a weak union. One half of the men were younger than 37 years compared with 53 years in the case of the leaders of weak bargainers. Their

44

relative youthfulness means that only a few of the presidents founded their unions. The large majority of presidents have worked their way up through an instructive apprenticeship. The younger leaders are not tainted by associations with the weak and dominated union of earlier years. They boast an impressive record of extra-union activities. The majority are active in politics and all of those in the study participate in various community, social, fraternal, athletic, and veterans organizations.

For example, the 47-year-old leader of a 2,000 member union recalled:

> "I joined when the union was formed in 1935. The company was running the union and it had no interest for me. When the company in 1940 refused our demand for paid holidays, I decided to get interested, and helped lead a quickie strike. . . . From 1942 to 1945 I served as a steward. Then I put in two years as an alternative Departmental Representative. In 1947 I was elected to the Executive Council and to the Grievance Committee as a Departmental Representative. From 1948 through 1951 I served as a representative both for my department and for the entire union on the subject of time-study and wages. Since 1952 I have led the entire show. . . . Union business takes three quarters of the time I spend in and outside of the plant."

This man also served as a union representative to the city's United Community Fund, and participated in the affairs of the Holy Name Society, the Catholic Youth Organization, and the local Democratic Club.

Another representative tale was offered by the president of a union of 38 oil depot employees.

> "I was not especially interested but I attended meetings regular. At nomination time I began kidding the boys about having a dinner dance. They nominated me! The union was so poor it disgusted me. Just booze after meetings, no real representation, and company-domination. I decided to straighten it up—and I've been working at it ever since."

Strong Unions

Such sentiments make it possible to understand the various successes of the strong unions.

Nor is it surprising to learn that the leaders of strong single-firm independent unions have a broad conception of trade union behavior. Two-thirds of the men believe labor should participate in politics and should give money to political candidates. A few of their unions endorse candidates for political office, and most other strong unions participate in the political activities of a statewide multi-union association. For example, a president of a 60-member union of paint company employees recalled:

> "We pushed a registration drive at first and got 90 percent registered. So we decided to take the next step and I spoke for the two Democratic candidates at a regular meeting. It didn't cause any trouble. . . . 99 percent of the men would have voted for them anyhow."

The president of a 200-member union in a lamp manufacturing plant told a more involved story:

> "Our employer got the nod for the Senate race and we were glad to back him. I went to other independent unions and tried to get support, but most of the presidents were afraid to push endorsements. . . . I spoke at meetings, however, and advertised that my union and the State Association of Independent Unions supported my man. . . . He paid for my lost time and expenses, and, even after his defeat, he set up a little meeting so the Governor and his wife could thank a bunch of us."

More recently, in 1961, the two presidents quoted above and several others were instrumental in lining up the support of independent unions behind an eventually victorious Democratic gubernatorial candidate.

In keeping with such political concern, the leaders of strong unions manifest pro-labor political attitudes. Unlike their weak union counterparts, the majority oppose right-to-work (or anti-union shop) laws, do not believe organized labor presently constitutes a monopoly threat to the economy, and express skepticism regarding McClellan Committee disclosures.

Strong Unions

Carefully managed complexity is the prime characteristic of the services of the strong unions. Endorsing a broad definition of unionism, the leaders of strong unions accept the complexity of their leadership tasks. In the matter of services, for example, the strong unions offer modest but on-going programs. Several of those studied engage in vigorous voter registration drives, and cooperate with management in the operation of an in-plant charity drive. Others subsidize the attendance of members at adult education classes in labor subjects and conduct successful weekend conferences on time-study and the like. They also hold occasional beer parties or fishing trips.

Social services, such as these parties, are not only recreational but are also a measure of accomplishment in the union's relations with management. Typical of pertinent quotations here was one from the president of a 38-man union of oil depot employees:

"We had our union picnic last Sunday. One hundred and fifteen people paid admission and thirty-five families were counted. . . . We were damn surprised when the Assistant Divisional Manager in Charge of Operations came all the way out from New York. Why, he even played ball with the guys and acted like one of us. I guess New York knows now that I am serious about my union, and they are starting to take us seriously, too."

The strong unions are also interested in providing personnel services (such as discount cards) and in supporting a public relations effort to disassociate their public image from that of the weak union. Resources, however, severely limit action in both regards.

The strong union's labor-management relations are complex, so much so that a third of the leaders interviewed had taken courses in labor subjects at adult education centers. In preparing for negotiations, half of the presidents use government data and consult with a labor lawyer and other union leaders. Several presidents subscribe to the publications of international unions, multi-union associations, and private labor services such as the Bureau of National Affairs.[4] A third of the presidents had benefited from plant, company, or industry-wide conferences of like unions, and half of them use annual reports and other company sources of data.

Reflecting careful preparations, the contracts of strong single-firm unions are slowly and warily drafted. None of the presidents sit and listen while two opposing lawyers settle the matter; nor do these presidents, like the head of one weak union, nod agreement while a company executive reads the contract of a sister plant. Rather, the full range of early morning sessions, strategic recesses, consultations in the hallway, and hurried notes around the bargaining table are employed. The strong union occasionally adds one tactic unique to the unaffiliated organization: the threat of affiliation. Several of these unions and none of their weak counterparts reported using this tactic. Some strong unions threaten to affiliate with an unsavory or powerful international union unless the new contract contains certain union demands or relations otherwise take a desired turn.[5]

With such preparations, negotiations, and tactics behind them, the presidents of strong bargainers show considerable confidence in their contracts. Most believe their wages and fringe benefits are better than those prevailing for comparable work in the area and industry. A comparison of their contract terms with data compiled by the Bureau of Labor Statistics confirms their appraisal.[6] Overall, the members of strong independent single-firm unions receive higher hourly earnings, have more paid holidays, and have longer vacation periods than other comparable workers in the area.

The strong unions complement their bargaining strength with considerable shop influence. They can negotiate such strategic matters as level of work performance, promotion to non-supervisory position and job content.[7] The large majority of the unions regularly meet with management to discuss plant problems. Half of them record their grievances and keep a careful account of the union's grievance history. None permit members to take grievances directly to management, thereby protecting the importance of the joint grievance machinery. While arbitration is not popular (it is thought to be costly and lengthy), several strong unions had resorted to it; and several had struck their employer at least once in the past. The strong union, in short, shows a sophisticated awareness of how to apply industrial pressure.[8]

The need to apply such pressure has many different roots, some involving common union-management differences such as contract matters, and others more intimately related to the independent union as such. An example of the latter was provided by the president of a 200-member union of lamp company employees who commented:

> "Since we're an independent union we go out of our way to give good service. The UAW or some other outfit would swallow us up overnight if we relaxed. The company generally understands, but occasionally forgets. Like what I mean is we can't use affiliation as a threat in negotiations. Hell, they're so angry at us now that they want us to affiliate. They know the UAW would not bother them the way we do. We give 100 percent service."

The leader of a 1,500-member union of chemical company employees offered this explanation of strained relations:

> "The company got through to our former union president. He had served for eight years and enjoyed lush personal arrangements with the supervisors. What's even worse, he began to talk about affiliation with a weak CIO outfit. I knocked him out of office in a very close election. His slate kept a few top jobs, however, and he still has a lot of friends. So the pressure on me is great. We have struck before and will strike again if the company doesn't catch on to my situation."

Other presidents traced strained relations to their isolation and lack of staff aid and "political" contracts.

This does not lead most presidents of strong unions to distrust or dislike the company or company men they dealt with. On the contrary, as Father Purcell suggests in his hypothesis of "dual loyalty," members of a union in an arms-length relationship have no special trouble respecting their employer if that respect is due.[9] Only a third of the strong union presidents believe the company abuses its power. Most hope to remain at their present jobs until they retire and most would accept a supervisory post if it were offered. The majority respect traditional managerial prerogatives, believing top management to be reasonable and effective. They credit the company with understanding the problems of a union officer.[10]

Typical of comments here was one offered by the president of a 1,700-member union of instrument company employees:

> "The company is applying more pressure now than usual, what with the recent conversion to piece rates and the crumby recession coming together. The company is putting the heat on, but we understand that it has to be done so we do not respond with heat. It would be a damn poor relationship if we did. Instead, we put pressure on our members to help the company improve its position. We ask the boys to correct poor working habits and improve production. . . . The company is very frank and cooperative. They even trust me with confidential information, and I know I can depend on them for political favors. The higher you go, the nicer you find them; but, with few exceptions, they're all pretty good guys."

This particular union had struck the employer in 1947 and again in 1953. With dues of $2.50 per member per month coming in from 1,700 members, it was in a better position than many others to sustain a work stoppage. It is characteristic of the able leaders of strong single-firm unions that industrial cooperation, rather than conflict, is the major concern.

The employer, for his part, is usually also concerned with cooperation. Nearly all interviewed were satisfied with their union-management relations, the temporary discomfort of conflict notwithstanding. They particularly value the unions' maneuverability, resourcefulness and integrity. Union maneuverability helps labor and management vary contract conditions according to business and economic conditions. Union resourcefulness means management can expect a documented case from the union in negotiations and can itself employ useful facts and figures. Union integrity encourages management to accept the union's word and to behave as if the union has the support of most shop members. Arms-length relationships apparently do not blind either side to the values inherent in the dealings of proved, capable, and mature parties.[11]

Moreover, arms-length relationships do not prevent the strong union from enjoying more rewards from joint union-employer undertakings than the weak ones do from employer paternalism. Proportionately more strong than weak unions participate in free company picnics, company suggestion plans, jointly-operated social and athletic clubs, and safety and accident programs. The unions' role in these programs adds, of course, to their already complex administrative tasks.

The government of the strong independent union is as efficient as dedicated men can make it. Among the responsibilities that weigh heavily on these blue-collar, part-time leaders is the care of treasuries ranging from $1,400, a minimum amount more than the wealthiest weak union's treasury, to $66,000. One union owned its own meeting hall, another was conducting a building drive, and a third was amassing a large welfare fund. These projects prosper without the costly overhead of professional administrators.[12] They are supported by a modest dues schedule, one higher than that of weak unions but lower than that of most international union locals. A majority of the strong unions charge $2.50 or more per member per month. This figure does not satisfy the leaders, and some campaign for an increase. They argue fervently that a strong union "just does not come cheap."

The number of meetings, like the size of the treasury, is related to the size of the union: the larger the union, the fewer the general meetings it holds and the greater its reliance on small monthly executive sessions. Nevertheless, proportionately more strong than weak unions hold monthly membership meetings. Similarly, although none of the strong unions achieve the 100 percent attendance claimed by some small weak unions, proportionately more strong than weak unions have a regular attendance of 25 percent or more of their membership.

The business at these meetings can get fairly involved. Discussion sometimes turns to the union's relations with other labor unions (most strong unions were in touch with neighboring unions, unaffiliated and international). Such discussions consider the fear that these relations could lead to an organizational raid. Many strong independents have beaten off raids in recent years, and the possibility of future conflict is a real one. Another frequent topic is the common problem of craft differentials. (Weak unions are generally spared this problem by their small size.) A few of the unions have recently won NLRB decisions preventing the severance of disgruntled craftsmen; two strong unions had been formed in 1960 as a result of an irresolvable craft squabble in the parent union, and dissension threatened in several other unions.

Analysis. The strong bargainer modifies the basic characteristics of the single-firm independent union which the weak bargainer epitomizes. Formalities are certainly not forced in place of the personal touch, but they are given more extensive use. A plant-orientation and a concentration on the employer are both supplemented by union concern with area or industry labor standards, labor legislation, and social reform. This concern helps liberalize the independent union's characteristically conservative ideology at the same time that it challenges the notion that big unions and big government are everywhere conspiring against these unions. The strong union's comparatively large size and urban location weaken its commitment to the notion of smallness as a virtue, and may even encourage new interest in affiliation as a means of augmenting strength.

Theoretically, such a strong independent union should prove a valid alternative for workers unimpressed with the international unions and with the weak single-firm unions. But an alternative must be known to decision-makers if they are to take it into account and this union is not known to the American working man. Paradoxically, this strong effective form of the single-firm union is even more obscure than the weak form.[13] It has figuratively had to use a hand-press and megaphone to do a publicity job that demands the equivalent of a printing factory and many loud speakers.

The bargaining tactics of the strong single-firm union demonstrate how inter-union competition and the threat of affili-

Strong Unions

ation can be turned to the worker's advantage. Its accomplishments suggest that professional or bureaucratic leadership and "intellectual" staff aid may not be necessary in all types of labor organization. Finally, and most importantly, its strength establishes that single-firm independent unions are as capable as any others of forcefully and fruitfully representing their members.

FOOTNOTES

1. The strong single-firm union is the overlooked exception to the generalization that single-firm unions are weak unions. Merton suggests: "More is learned from the single success than from multiple failures. A single success proves it can be done. Therefore it is necessary only to learn what made it work." Merton, Robert K., *Social Theory and Social Structure* (Glencoe, Ill.: The Free Press, 1st edition, 1949), pp. 194-195.

2. For example, a 1959 study of a defunct single-firm union of 2,000 refinery workers suggests that its " 'blood and guts' approach was derived at least in part from the fact that these individuals had experienced some of the black days of union-management relations; had participated in the struggle for more power; had persevered to taste the fruits of victory." Donnelly, Margaret E., "Industrial Relocation: A Branch of the Pattern of Industry-Community Relationships" (Unpublished Doctoral Dissertation, Fordham University, 1959), pp. 113, 121.

3. Marshall notes that "The image that Esso attempts to create of being a good employer makes it vulnerable to worker protest, a fact which has not escaped [the union] leaders; branch managers are probably more vulnerable to such embarrassing episodes than local managers responsible only to stockholders." Marshall, F. Ray, "Independent Unions in the Gulf Coast Petroleum Refining Industry—The Esso Experience," *Labor Law Journal* (September, 1961), p. 834. For a provocative discussion of the finding that "the larger the company and the greater the spread of stock ownership, the more managers perceive common interest with the union," see Dent, James K. and De La Paz, Romeo, "Union Security and Management Attitudes," *Personnel Psychology*, 14 (Summer, 1961), pp. 178-179.

4. Dubin believes that one of the most significant latent functions of unions is the union's mechanism for collective social mobility through collective bargaining. The mechanism entails invidious comparisons made by unions between their standing and the standing of other labor groups in the labor market. The mechanism is common to the strong and not to the weak single-firm union. See Dubin, Robert, "Power and Union-Management Relations," *Administrative Science Quarterly*, 2 (June, 1957), pp. 60-82.

5. The threat provides a poll of the attitude of the membership towards affiliation and towards particular international unions, and a measure of the employer's commitment to the status quo.

6. The contract terms of the strong unions were compared with terms reported in U.S. Department of Labor, *Occupational Wage Survey: Newark and Jersey City, New Jersey: February 1960* (Washington, D.C.:

Strong Unions

veryhighBureau of Labor Statistics, Bulletin No. 1265-28). See also Shostak, Arthur, "The Role and Viability of the Single-Firm Unaffiliated Union" (Unpublished Doctoral Dissertation, Princeton University, 1961).

7. A 1960 study takes as evidence of apparently "firm and assured" union status the fact that "in addition to the traditional subjects of wages, hours, and working conditions, the union negotiated over a wide variety of topics directly related to the job territory. . . ." Derber, Milton, *et al., The Local Union-Management Relationship* (Urbana, Ill.: Institute of Labor and Industrial Relations, University of Illinois, 1960), p. 49. Dubin suggests that "where functions are performed jointly, then the power is more diffuse than would be true if only one party performed them." Dubin, Robert, "A Theory of Conflict and Power in Union-Management Relations," *Industrial and Labor Relations Review,* 13 (July, 1960), p. 507.

8. Galbraith suggests that "the sound and fury which so commonly marks our collective bargaining tells nothing of the state of rapport in our labor relations. They show only that the process of collective bargaining is being conducted normally." Galbraith, John Kenneth, *Economics and the Art of Controversy* (New York: Vintage Books, 1959), p. 20.

9. The hypothesis was first advanced in Purcell, Theodore V., S.J., *The Worker Speaks His Mind on Company and Union* (Cambridge, Mass.: Harvard University Press, 1953). A critical appraisal is available in "Dual Allegiance to Union and Management: A Symposium," *Personnel Psychology,* 7 (Spring, 1954), pp. 41-81; England, George W., "Dual Allegiance to Company and Union," *Personnel Administration,* March-April 1960, pp. 20-25. The most recent literature on the subject is reviewed and the concept reexamined in Purcell, Theodore V., S.J., *Blue-Collar Man* (Cambridge, Mass.: Harvard University Press, 1960).

10. The sympathy of the leaders of strong single-firm unions for the employers they deal with probably stems from a situation of "stable equilibrium between the two players, not merely because each is satisfying the expectations of the other, but because each is helping the other to satisfy the expectations of some *third* party." Gouldner, Alvin, *Wildcat Strike* (Yellow Springs, Ohio: The Antioch Press, 1954), p. 56. See also the explanation of a "constructive" relationship available in Harbison, Frederick H., *Patterns of Union Management Relations* (Chicago, Ill.: Science Research Associates, 1947), pp. 205, 211.

11. The situation of the strong single-firm union closely resembles a pattern of local union relations which reflects "moderate union influence, absence of pressure, favorable attitudes, friendly emotional tone, ability to settle negotiations without outside assistance, rapid grievance settlement, low reliance on past practice, and a willingness to make concessions to the other side." At times, however, this pattern, labelled "moderate joint participation," gives way to one labelled "aggression and resistance"; the weak single-firm union knows only the pattern called "quiescence." See Derber, *et al., ibid.,* p. 114. See also the description of environmental forces that permit industrial peace in National Planning Association, *Causes of Industrial Peace Under Collective Bargaining* (Washington, D.C., NPA, 1953).

12. Salaries are low for part-time leaders; the range is between $100 for a union of 650 members to $1,440 annually for a union of 1,500 members. Six blue-collar and two white-collar unions had full-time offi-

cers; in some other unions the time allowed off plant work for union work approached 40 hours. Significantly, only a few single-firm unions sought super-seniority for their leaders who are, after all, basically co-workers, and only one union permitted a dues refund to officers. This probably reflects a democratic ethos and the leader's political sensitivity of the leaders.

13. Unfortunately it is not possible to say how many of the nation's single-firm unions are strong unions, and to know whether the number is changing. One-half of the writer's sample were strong unions; Walton's study of eleven white-collar engineering unions concludes that five or six involve a containment-aggression pattern, one is engaged in continuing conflict, and the remainder have entered a pattern of accommodation. See Walton, Richard E., *The Impact of the Professional Engineering Union* (Boston, Mass.: Harvard University, 1961), pp. 34-36. Note that Walton is an uneven guide in this matter because he does not indicate exactly how many of the eleven unions were or were not single-firm organizations, and what were the relations of the former alone.

VI. UNIONS OF WHITE-COLLAR WORKERS

VARIOUS attractions of the independent unions such as home-rule, low dues, plant orientation, and industrial harmony are not lost on white-collar workers. A small segment of the white-collar non-professional labor force is organized in single-firm unions in the telephone, utility, petroleum, and manufacturing industries.[1] Indeed, in the telephone industry forty or so single-firm independent unions with about 187,000 members constitute the industry's second largest union force (a rival international union is considerably larger).[2] These organizations of non-professional employees are particularly interesting because they organize a section of the work force which is traditionally hostile to unionism.[3]

Basic Characteristics and Appeal. Blue-collar and white-collar single-firm unions share certain features. Both are confined to the employees of a single employer and include collective bargaining among their other functions. A white-collar membership results in no major alteration of the single-firm union's basic characteristics.[4] Like its blue-collar counterpart, the white-collar union is generally "person-based," plant (office)-oriented, employer centered, conservative, and motivated by the unique ideology of these unions. Furthermore, these five characteristics uniquely complement special interests of most office employees.

Single-firm independent unions of office workers pay particular attention to preserving informal union procedures. This is largely in response to pressure for "person-based" methods from the majority of women in the white-collar unions. These women, mostly young, temporary employees, prefer friendly face-to-face relations to impersonal procedures. They are encouraged in this by the small size of many offices, generally warm employer-employee relations and the active grapevine of most offices.

Independent unions of white-collar workers are office-oriented. This is not surprising as there is no "labor movement" of white-collar workers to compete with the office for their at-

56

tention, and their pride in white-collar and unaffiliated status discourages any interest in the large blue-collar international unions. Nor are the white-collar unions interested in pursuing political or community activities outside of the office. This may reflect after-work participation in other organizations or a disinterest in all but social activities on the part of young men and women. There is also a lack of consensus on appropriate community interests because of the geographic dispersion of branch offices and the residences of employees.

These unions of office workers are employer-centered. This characteristic complements the fact that such employees hope to move eventually into management positions and are intent on learning everything about management that might help them secure a promotion. A sharp focus on the employer complements a marked affinity between the similarly dressed, educated, and motivated employees and employer.[5] Widespread concern with technological displacement also encourages a characteristic concern with the employer's every financial, managerial, scientific, and public relations development.

A conservative orientation is clearly discernible in most white-collar unions. Conservative ways seem natural to status-anxious, upwardly-mobile middle-class office employees, most of whom place a very high value on respectability, appearance, and harmony.[6] These employees are decidedly adverse to daring union maneuvers, strike threats, harsh bargaining, or strained employer-employee relations. They prefer time-honored ways and are further encouraged in this conservatism by the knowledge that union militance does not impress strike-proof employers. Telephone companies, for example, are automated to a point that defies disturbance by a labor walkout.[7]

Finally, white-collar unions adapt the basic ideology of independent unions to fit their particular circumstances. Along with blue-collar members of single-firm unions, their members believe Big Unions and Big Government conspire against independent unions, and they agree that this unfair conspiracy excuses many shortcomings of their unions and hides much of the promise.[8] They do not completely agree, however, with the characteristic championing of small organizations. Some of the white-collar unions are themselves large organizations and many of them bargain with large and impressive employers in the telephone and utility industries. Nevertheless, since rival international unions are even larger, there is still room for qualified censure of large organizations. The basic ideology is modified but it is recognizable, and the modification complements the white-collar employees' grudging admiration of efficient giants and their deep-set dislike of the impersonality associated with such giants.[9]

Union Types. The independent union of office workers resembles the blue-collar union in more than structural and "personality" characteristics; it also exists in the same two major varieties, namely, as a weak union and as a strong union. Three case studies help make this clear: the cases involve a weak single-firm union of 44 oil depot office workers, a weak union of 1,900 phone company employees, and a strong union of 1,700 utility company office workers.

The small union was confined to 44 clerks and secretaries in a petroleum company depot. Even though it was only 15 years old, its middle-aged male president had no idea why or how it was founded. The union charged members 25 cents a month, and used dues receipts to pay two dollars rent annually to the company for the right to hold monthly meetings in the office during the employee lunch hour. One-third of the members were women; so, while the union conducted no political, community, personal, educational, or public relations activities, it made a point of conducting one dinner-dance every year, an event which regularly exhausted its treasury. Labor-management relations were very cordial, and the union felt no need for bargaining research or the recording of grievances. Nor did it bother to maintain relations with a weak blue-collar union in the same depot, though it occasionally contacted small white-collar unions in other depots of the same petroleum company. The president of the union had no knowledge of the state's celebrated multi-union association and no knowledge of any national association. When asked what the major purpose of the union was, the president explained: "We keep this union together in order to freeze out an outside organization."[10]

The second of the three white-collar unions was a weak organization of 1,900 phone operators and clerical and sales employees. It had been formed in 1928 as a company-sponsored employee association and had never fully outgrown a dependency on the employer for paternalistic concessions. In contrast, the third union, a strong organization of 1,700 white-collar employees of an electric and gas company, had been organized in 1942 despite employer opposition and had never been subject to excessive influence by the employer.

The two large unions differed not only in age and reasons for formation, but in most other crucial aspects. Sixty-five per cent of the weak union's members were women as compared with 17 per cent of the strong union's members. Most of the women in the weak union were young recent high-school graduates. According to the male president of the phone company union:

> "The girls make a big difference in union policies. They are thinking of marriage, and not of union services. . . . They make us less strike prone. . . . Also, the company is very selective, and many of the girls have relatives in the ranks of management. . . . These girls do not have a career perspective. They want wage gains here and now, and they don't want to push for better pension allotments. This splits the union into two factions, and between the demands of the girls and the steady workers we must spread our bargaining demands pretty thin. . . ."

The membership of the two unions also differed in career perspective; fewer telephone workers than utility workers planned to make a career of their employment and fewer telephone union members desired maximum employee protection and rewards.

Union activities in the two organizations differed greatly. With dues of $1.25 a month and gross receipts in 1959 of only $18,000, the telephone union had a limited treasury, one that barely sustained a union newspaper and low-cost legal counsel to members. It sponsored no political, personal, social, community, educational or public relations activities.[11] The utility firm union levied dues of $2.25 a month and collected nearly $50,000 in 1958; another $3,000 was received in dividends and interest from securities. With these funds, the strong union sponsored all-day conferences on labor contract and grievance procedure and sent representatives to labor relations conferences conducted by various universities. It participated in the educational activities of a state multi-union association, and paid the registration fee of any member going to an accredited labor school. It also raised and contributed several thousand dollars to help complete a labor studies center at a nearby university and paid the operating expenses of an amateur theatrical group which performed at Veterans Hospitals. In 1960-1961 the union vigorously supported passage of a state college bond issue, backed candidates endorsed by the state multi-union association, and strongly urged members to register and vote. At the union's urging, the company had provided Asian flu inoculations and considered a polio vaccination program. Other union activities included picnics and dances, and an annual day-long convention of several hundred delegates from all parts of the state.

Labor-management relations distinguished between the two unions and accurately reflected their position relative to a powerful employer. The weak union of telephone company workers sent a part-time president against full-time experienced company negotiators. A pattern-settlement was the rule, the pattern being set by other companies in the A.T.&T. organization or "sphere of influence." The union generally went along with the company for members believed the company shared its profits equitably if the company had had a "good year." Since the company's financial report was merged with that of A.T.&T., the weak union trusted the company to judge whether the previous year had been profitable and how profitable it had been.[12]

Negotiations between the strong union of utility employees and the company also involved a pattern-settlement but one strengthened by the union's special efforts. The union nominally benefited from a tandem collective-bargaining relationship that predated its existence. That is, the labor contract won by a 6,000-member blue-collar local of utility workers largely determined the independent union's own contract gains. This had resulted over the years in average and often better-than-average terms for the independent compared with other contracts in the area. Not satisfied with this only, the union used rigorous preparation for negotiations, a full-time president and able legal counsel, and the calculated development of company respect to push beyond wage gains from the tandem relationship. The union had secured:

> ". . . the formalization of the principle of equal pay for equal work. . . . The filling of jobs by formula, not favoritism. . . . Separation of Social Security from the [company's] Pension Plan. . . . Increases in Group Insurance. . . . A workable 'disability downgrading formula.' . . . Company aid to education for the employees."

Negotiators also sought a shorter workweek, a program for early retirement, a widows' pension fund, and a program to soften the effects of automation. All of these progressive demands went beyond the tandem bargaining relationship.

Not surprisingly, the weak union had very little influence in shop affairs. According to its president it negotiated only four of twenty standard subjects of bargaining. It won only half of the few grievances it processed, had never gone to arbitration and had never sanctioned a work stoppage. The president of the phone company union explained:

> "The company definitely has a Big Brother policy, but we are beginning to stand up to it. . . . I will concede that the company wields a big stick, but they give us a good contract. We are sensitive to what the company is doing. That's it, we are not dominated—but we are sensitive to the company."

On the surface, the record of the strong union was similar to that of the weak union, but appearances were deceiving. The strong organization won only half of its grievances, not because it preferred to let the company police the grievance machinery but because the company only brought up "sure" things. The union avoided arbitration, not because of inexperience or fear of offending the company, but because arbitration was thought too costly and lengthy. It had never struck the company but it did pay $13,000 in out-of-work benefits to members who stayed home during a 1959 strike of another union in the company.

Unions of White-Collar Workers

Finally, the two unions of office workers differed in their interest in affiliation. The telephone workers were regularly wooed by the Communications Workers of America and the International Brotherhood of Electrical Workers. The president reported there was no definite move afoot to affiliate, but "the future is up in the air." The utility workers were also sought by various international unions. Nevertheless, its president believed that "not even one per cent of the members were pro-affiliation."[13]

Employers and the White-Collar Single-firm Union. Management has the same opinions of both blue- and white-collar unaffiliated unions. For example, the manager who dealt with the weak union of 44 oil depot employees explained:

> "The people you deal with representing the union are people you know. Everybody has basically the same interests; a good job, fair treatment, and good working conditions. . . . Nobody has to worry about outside ills, things like goon squads, graft, or corruption. The problems we deal with are our own. And we can deal quickly with them."

The specialist who negotiated with the weak union of 1,900 phone company employees added that it was an advantage not to have to worry about a parent international. The company representative who bargained with the strong union of 1,700 white-collar employees of a utility company valued dealing with an employee union leader, rather than a professional unionist. The employee was judged to be more sympathetic to the company, and to know and appreciate the company from past service.

Though these advantages and others far outweigh shortcomings, white-collar unions had several disadvantages from the company's standpoint. While the oil depot manager could not think of a single complaint with his small weak union, the phone industry union was criticized on four counts. The company felt the union's limited knowledge of labor relations elsewhere deprived it of valuable perspective and its poor treasury compelled it to settle for inadequate counsel. It accused the union of denying women members equal representation, and claimed that resentment of this disturbed the calm atmosphere the company cherished. The company also thought the union abused the grievance machinery to impress members with its militance. The utility company representative was disappointed with two aspects of his white-collar union. He felt that union democracy was overstressed and that this would not "let the dust settle around certain disputes." Union democracy also meant a frequent turnover in leadership forcing the company to "re-educate the new bigwigs," an expensive and trying project.

All three company representatives insisted that the union they dealt with generally did a fair and proper job of representing and rewarding members. Typical was the analysis offered by the phone company labor specialist:

> "This company protects its employees. We could really handle the union if we chose to, what with its amateur leaders and its apathetic members. But we do not choose to. The union helps us keep in touch with our employees and we help the union keep alive. . . . We know the union could not strike in a million years. It must settle on time. The company could take advantage of this but we protect the union instead by keeping the final settlement on a par with the competition . . . the union gives the best possible representation for the cheapest possible dues."

The company representatives claimed they did not have excessive influence over the union they dealt with. The oil depot manager vigorously insisted the company never interfered in the choice of a union leader. He added: "We are very conscious of NLRB rulings in this area. We bend over backwards to see that there is no domination and no patronage." The phone company labor specialist characterized the company as a "Big Brother" to the weak union, but argued that:

> ". . . our policy is hands off. And we can document this. We are not in control, although the union did appreciate the free office space and stenographic help we used to give. Today we are independent of one another and we have nuisance grievances and an occasional arbitration

case to prove it. Hell, we'd like the union to quiet the girls by putting more women on its executive council, but we have not said so. It would be taking liberties with their private affairs for us to say anything."

Similarly, the utility company representative denied having excessive influence over union affairs. He explained that factionalism in the strong union discouraged anything but proper relations, although, "as it is a white collar outfit, we all know it could never handle a strike."

Inter-Union Relations. While single-firm unions of non-professional office workers are generally office-oriented, circumstances compel considerable modification of this basic characteristic. Pattern-bargaining predominates in the telephone, utility, chemical, petroleum, and other industries. This encourages information-sharing arrangements between related single-firm independent unions and even between such unions and local unions. The white-collar unions are isolated organizations as unions of rarely organized office workers. This isolation encourages them to seek out the company of one another and even of similar blue-collar unions.[14] The white-collar unions are confronted by able and interested raiders. Potential or actual harassment encourages contact between related independent unions and membership in multi-union associations.

The history of associations of white-collar unions has not been a particularly happy one. It was highlighted by the conversion in 1947 of 46 phone industry independent unions in a multi-union association into locals of a powerful new international union. In 1939, the National Federation of Telephone Workers (NFTW) was formed by 27 single-firm unions representing 92,000 Bell System employees.[15] The dominant labor bloc in the industry, NFTW grew considerably over the years. It made some gains in organizing new unions, conducting educational programs, and protecting the legislative interests of phone workers. Indeed, it became a national spokesman for all single-firm unions and was the first such organization to win recognition on the War Labor Board and on a wartime industry-union committee. However, NFTW was considerably less successful in winning cooperation or bargaining gains from the phone companies. A breakdown in union-management relations in 1947 helped precipitate an unprecedented 30-day strike of 300,000 NFTW members. According to a former NFTW officer:

"... the basic weakness of the organization revealed itself. The basic weakness was this autonomy which had been guaranteed forever, and which at that time still existed, because after so many weeks of a strike our unions started to sign off as they saw fit and our strike did collapse because of the autonomy of the unions which belonged to the NFTW. This autonomy came to the fore, and the entire solidarity of the telephone workers was weakened by the independent unions belonging to the NFTW signing their separate contracts."[16]

On conclusion of this generally unsuccessful strike, 46 affiliates of the Federation representing 200,000 employees transformed NFTW into an international union.[17] In due course this union, the Communications Workers of America, affiliated with the CIO and later with the AFL-CIO. It has since come to dominate the union side of the industry.

The leading single-firm union federation in the telephone industry is the Alliance of Independent Telephone Unions. It includes twelve unions representing over 125,000 employees of Bell System Companies operating in New York, Pennsylvania, and seven other Northeastern states.[18] Among its more noteworthy moves has been its use of the ownership of A.T.&T. shares to allow it to present resolutions at annual stockholder meetings.[19] Another noteworthy single-firm union organization is the Federation of Westinghouse Independent Salaried Unions, a company-wide council representing office workers at 30 separate locations.[20] White-collar independent unions also participate in a New Jersey state association and city-wide associations in Rochester, New York, and Milwaukee, Wisconsin.

The recent history of independent union encounters with internationals is not particularly auspicious. It contains a spectacular 1960 victory by the Communications Workers of America (AFL-CIO) over two twenty-four year old telephone industry unions with a total of 24,000 members. As the culmination of a five-year effort, the victory brought the largest such gain for the Communications Workers since the 1940's, and the largest gain for any international union since the 1955 merger of the AFL and CIO. The raid demonstrated the seriousness of the international's efforts and the very high stakes involved.[21]

Relations between the Communications Workers and phone industry independent unions are possibly more strained than any existing between an international union and the unaffiliated unions in its jurisdiction. This reflects their active disagreement over appropriate government policy toward Bell System labor relations.[22] According to a student of the industry, the 1947 War Labor Board finding concerning Bell System labor relations still appears applicable in the 1960's. The Board had characterized the wage structure of the Bell System as a "function both of basic area wage levels and the unifying influence of the closely knit Bell System." Independent unions seek to reinforce and if possible, to enlarge regional differentials. They want government aid in loosening the "unifying influence" of the American Telephone and Telegraph Company over the "closely knit Bell System." International unions, on the other hand, particularly the Communications Workers, want government aid in forcing A.T.&T. to act as the real employer and bargain with unions on a national basis. This difference of opinion on government policy runs very deep, and effectively impedes friendly relations between the single-firm unions in the phone industry and the international.[23]

Unlike the single-firm union of blue-collar workers, the union of white-collar office employees is still trying to justify its existence. Checked by powerful and paternalistic employers, the conservatism of a predominantly female membership, and the fact that only ten percent of all office employees are unionized, the single-firm union makes an understandably weak showing. On the other hand, the union does reflect certain character-

Unions of White-Collar Workers

istics of white-collar employees themselves who, for example, focus on their employer and the office rather than on the "labor movement." In this fashion, the single-firm union of white-collar employees offers itself as a promising alternative to organization by international unions or to no organization at all. The persistence of the single-firm unions despite considerable hardship counsels new respect for the union's wide appeal, its staying power and its prospects.

FOOTNOTES

1. Single-firm unions of office workers, bank tellers, meter readers, phone operators, and technicians are known to the writer. They appear younger than their blue-collar counterparts and are somewhat less harassed by raiders. Note that the writer will not use the comparatively rich literature available on single-firm unions of teachers, government employees, and public nurses, as this study is restricted to unions in private enterprise.

2. In 1960, the Communications Workers of America (AFL-CIO) reported that there were 43 single-firm independent unions representing about 187,000 Bell System workers. All but one of these unions represented only segments or departments of a particular company. Private correspondence, August 29, 1960. In 1960, the CWA (AFL-CIO) claimed 259,917 members. U.S. Department of Labor, *Directory of National and International Labor Unions in the United States, 1961* (Washington, D.C.: Bureau of Labor Statistics, Bulletin 1320, March, 1962), p. 17. More recently the CWA (AFL-CIO) defeated and absorbed two single-firm unions with a combined membership of 24,000. However, it has also lost members to the never-ending process of automation. See "CWA Chalks Up Two Big Election Victories in N. Y.," *CWA News*, April, 1961, p. 1; Beirne, Joseph A., "The Job Revolution in Telephones," *IUD Digest*, Summer 1959, pp. 23-27.

3. The Bureau of Labor Statistics estimates that only about 12 per cent of American union members are in the white-collar ranks (or 2,200,000 workers). U.S. Department of Labor, *Directory of National and International Labor Unions in the United States, 1961, op. cit.*, p. 50. "A National Office Management Association survey indicates that the effort to organize the white-collar worker has made only a 3 per cent gain in the past ten years." *Dun's Review and Modern Industry*, May, 1961, p. 83.

4. The similarity in basic characteristics of both blue- and white-collar single-firm unions is especially striking in light of great differences in their members: "White-collar workers' education and income are in general higher than those of any other group in the labor force, and they enjoy greater job security than other workers. They experience little unemployment, generally are paid a salary rather than an hourly wage, and receive more liberal paid vacations and holidays and sick leave than other workers." Barry, Carol A., "White-Collar Employment: I—Trends and Structure," *Monthly Labor Review*, 84 (January, 1961), p. 11. The perma-

67

nence of difference is in doubt: See for example, Brooks, Tom, "Bleaching the Blue Collar," *Dun's Review and Modern Industry*, January, 1962, pp. 58, 60-64. See also *Labor Looks at the White Collar Worker* (Washington, D.C.: Industrial Union Department, AFL-CIO, 1957).

5. Mills observes, however, that: ". . . there is fear and even hatred of the boss. In fact, loyalty to management, advanced by white-collar employees, is often, unknown even to them, an insecure cover-up for fear of reprisal." Mills, C. Wright, *White Collar* (New York: Oxford University Press, 1956), p. 305. Bruner notes a "tendency among white-collar workers to want to look at both sides of the argument about unions—the union's side *and* the company's side. . . ." Bruner, Dick, "Why White Collar Workers Can't Be Organized," *Harpers*, August, 1957, pp. 44-50.

6. Dowd writes: "The white collar worker is likely to focus on the grievances surrounding his job—petty except for his fear of unemployment—and on his relatively low pay. These are precisely the areas in which business unionism is able to operate most effectively. The white collar worker's job is likely to bore, to frustrate, to irritate—not to outrage him. And, whatever the reality may be, there usually remains some vague hope of upward job mobility associated with white collar work." Dowd, Douglas F., "The White Collar Worker," *American Labor in Midpassage*, Bert Cochran, ed. (New York: Monthly Review Press, 1959), pp. 125-132.

7. Joseph Beirne, President of the CWA (AFL-CIO) frankly suggests that in the telephone industry "the use of a union's ultimate economic weapon—the strike—needs to be re-evaluated in terms of the new workforce. When fewer and fewer people are actually engaged in providing the direct service to the customer and more and more are involved in auxiliary functions, how effectively can you halt production? This, coupled with 95 per cent local dial service and 80 per cent long distance call dialing, suggests a pretty serious situation collective-bargaining-wise." Beirne, Joseph A., *op. cit.*, p. 24. Similarly, in congressional testimony the president of an association of 11 single-firm unions representing 125,000 Bell System employees conceded "a complete loss of power to combat this robot-like giant [automation] which could keep the telephone business going in the face of almost any kind of strike." Alliance of Independent Telephone Unions, *Statement of President Robert R. Montgomery, Jr., on June 12, 1961 before the House Subcommittee on Automation and Energy Resources* (Mimeographed).

8. For a thorough discussion of white-collar mentality, see Mills, C. Wright, *op. cit.*; Strauss, George, "White-Collar Unions are Different," *Harvard Business Review*, 32 (September-October, 1954), pp. 73-82; Dowd, Douglas, *op. cit.*, Bruner, Dick, *op. cit.*, Brooks, Tom, *op. cit.*

9. A representative of an international union of white-collar workers reports that as the number of clerical workers in large-scale offices has increased, their jobs have become "rationalized, diluted, standardized, and routinized. They are expected to exercise less judgment and initiative and at the same time are subjected to the kind of bureaucratic regimentation which the man on the assembly line had long been plagued with. . . . Under such circumstances, what happens to the white-collar worker's closeness to and identification with management, and his own sense of

Unions of White-Collar Workers

status and importance?" McKinstry, Lois, "The Wilting White Collar," in *Labor Looks at the White Collar Worker, op. cit.*, p. 33.

10. See Chapter 3, "A Comparison of the Union and the Local," for an extended discussion of the attributes of a powerless labor organization. It is not yet possible to say to what extent white-collar unions can generally be found alongside blue-collar single-firm unions, and it is not known whether the situation of one can deviate from that of the other.

11. A lack of union activities bears little relationship to the nature of the industry and the employees it attracts. For an account of a local union of telephone employees that boasts a very active program, see Nurnberger, T. S., "Experiences with White-Collar Unions," *Addresses on Industrial Relations: 1959 Series*, Gretchen M. Foster, *et al.*, eds. (Ann Arbor, Michigan: Bureau of Industrial Relations, University of Michigan, Bulletin No. 27, 1960), Address No. 15, pp. 14-26.

12. In fairness it should be noted that Troy's evaluation of the contracts of single-firm and of international unions in the telephone industry leads him to conclude that terms are as good or better in the former's agreements. Troy adds that "collective bargaining does not seem to be an important factor in explaining the existing wage structure of the Bell System. Instead, economic factors and wartime regulation of wages appear to be the variables most responsible." Troy, Leo, "Local Independent and National Unions: Competitive Labor Organizations," *The Journal of Political Economy*, LXVIII (October, 1960), pp. 493-494.

13. Detailed accounts of the single-firm unions of utility company and telephone company employees are available in Shostak, Arthur, "The Role and Viability of the Single-Firm Unaffiliated Union" (Unpublished Doctoral Dissertation, Princeton University, 1961); Troy, Leo, *Local Independent Unionism: Two Case Studies* (New Brunswick, N.J.: Institute of Management and Labor Relations, Rutgers—The State University, 1961). For relatively rare recognition by single-firm unions that weak organizations exist, see *UTU News*, April, 1960; "Bell Companies Like Weak Unions: Some Still Fighting On," *The Commentator* (Commercial Telephone Workers of New Jersey), July, 1960, pp. 2, 4.

14. The strong union of utility workers previously described is the only white-collar union in a state-wide association of single-firm unions. This fact casts doubt on the argument that white-collar employees categorically reject dealings with blue-collar unions.

15. Information on the National Federation of Telephone Workers is taken from Barbash, Jack, *Unions and Telephones* (New York: Harper & Brothers, 1952). See also *Let's Do It Together* (Washington, D.C.: Communications Workers of America, AFL-CIO).

16. U.S. Congress, Senate, Subcommittee on Labor and Public Welfare, *Hearings, Labor-Management Relations in the Bell Telephone System*, 81st Congress, 2nd Session, 1950, pp. 49-50. Testimony of Joseph Beirne, now President of the CWA (AFL-CIO).

17. The transformation of NFTW into CWA entailed subjecting the affiliates to the authority of the national convention. "Taking an almost unprecedented step, the NFTW unions voluntarily gave up their autonomy in the interests of the whole membership." *Let's Do it Together, op. cit.*, p. 4. See also Chapter 8, "The Associations of Single-Firm Independent Unions."

18. On the Alliance, see *Statement of President . . . , op. cit.* Note that

Unions of White-Collar Workers

as in the case of associations of blue-collar single-firm unions, membership figures offered by the Alliance are suspect: A June, 1961 claim mentions 125,000 Bell System employees while an August, 1961 article mentions only 80,000. See *Statement* . . . , *ibid.*, and *The Commentator* (Commercial Telephone Workers of New Jersey), August, 1961, p. 1.

19. Tilove asks: "What, if anything, have unions done about the potentialities for corporate influence in the pension funds they help to administer? . . . The unions have made no attempt to use this potential power. . . . There are some exceptions. . . . The Alliance of Independent Telephone Unions owns a number of shares in A.T.&T., which it has used for over ten years to present resolutions at annual meetings to eliminate the deduction of one-half of the Social Security benefit from the A.T.&T. pension." Tilove, Robert, *Pension Funds and Economic Freedom* (New York: Fund for the Republic, 1959), p. 70. This is one of the only examples of initiative the writer discovered in the entire body of literature on blue- and white-collar single-firm unions (excluding those unions composed of engineers).

20. On the Federation, see Bollens, Leo F., *White-Collar or Noose: The Occupation of Millions* (New York: North River Press, 1947); Federation of Westinghouse Independent Salaried Unions, *The Regulator*, 1946-1962. The Federation is unique for its intra-company organizing campaign, its successful integration of clerical and engineering personnel, and its strained labor relations.

21. For accounts of the victory, see *CWA News, op. cit.*; "CWA Rings the Bell," *John Herling's Labor Letter*, March 11, 1961; *New York Times*, March 8, 1961; "AFL-CIO Phone Union Breaks 24-Year Sway of Independent," *Business Week*, March 18, 1961, p. 120.

22. A discussion of the difference in policy between single-firm unions and the CWA is available in Troy, Leo, *op. cit.* See also U.S. Congress, Senate, Subcommittee on Labor and Public Welfare, *Hearings Labor-Management Relations in the Bell Telephone System, op. cit.*; pp. 521-559; *UTU News* (United Telephone Organization), 1956-1960, especially Mayer, Henry, "The Dilemma of Telephone Workers," *UTU News*, January 1960, p. 11. See also Chapter 9, "Relations with the Internationals: Competition and Cooperation."

23. CWA is also hampered in its affiliation efforts by the charge that the contract pattern it promotes nationally often favors its better-organized low-wage areas over less well-organized high-wage areas. Indeed, the persistence of single-firm unions in high-wage areas is largely attributable to this fear. CWA denies the charge and insists that only the companies benefit from disunity: they "force poorer contracts upon CWA by undercutting [its] bargaining position in quickly reached settlements with other organizations. . . . By playing upon our lack of unity, the corporations have been able to deny us gains that should rightfully have been won long ago." *Let's Do it Together, op. cit.*, p. 16.

VII. UNIONS OF ENGINEERS

THE nation's single-firm unions exist only among one type of professional, the engineer employed in industry.[1] Approximately ten unions represent nine thousand engineers and technicians of such firms as General Electric, Lockheed Aircraft Corporation, RCA, Standard Oil Company of Indiana, Westinghouse, and others. The single-firm unions constitute the second largest union force among engineers; the international unions represent only 7,500 professionals while the multi-firm independent unions may represent 23,500 engineers and technicians.[2] The single-firm unions warrant attention for this and three other reasons: Their plight illustrates problems faced by single-firm unions regardless of the type of member involved. Their structure illustrates the degree to which they can adapt to special circumstances. And, their situation sheds light on the likelihood of their expansion into the fastest growing and least well-organized sector of the labor force.

Background. Like many blue-collar counterparts, single-firm independent unions of engineers frequently originated in a defensive move rather than in a grievance-based situation. Most of the unions were formed shortly after World War II by engineers anxious to avoid inclusion in the collective-bargaining units of powerful blue-collar internationals.[3] The Taft-Hartley Act of 1947 lessened the threat to engineers of unwilling inclusion by guaranteeing them a vote and a veto in the matter.[4]

A few single-firm unions of engineers were organized after 1947 as a result of growing discontent with employment conditions. This discontent focused on rather specific complaints, many of which persist to this day and help explain the continued persistence of the unions:

> "Loss of economic position in comparison with labor. No premium pay for overtime. Too little personal recognition by supervisors. Use of engineers for semi-technical jobs. Lack of planning for the development of young engineers to increase their effectiveness and to utilize their particular talents. Inadequate measures taken to prevent

71

loss of dignity, and failure to maintain professional standing. Failure to provide adequate channels of two-way communications. Inadequate and undesirable offices. Lack of secretarial and drafting assistance. Punching time clocks. Checking by plant guards when coming in late."[5]

While some factors have left the list, new complaints have been added. While particular emphases may have changed over the intervening years, the tone of the grievances is still an accurate reflection of the attitudes of many engineer employees.

Even though formed as a result of grievances, the younger organizations resembled older independent unions of engineers in their eagerness to establish that unionization presented no threat to management. To this end, the younger unions adopted what Walton calls the "educate-management" approach.[6] They stressed those goals of engineers that coincided with company objectives and they interpreted the union's job as one of education and persuasion:

"We have certain needs; and these are reasonable needs; therefore, all we have to do is educate management regarding our problems; being comprised of reasonable men management will set about to solve the problems."[7]

In fact, however, the "educate-management" approach exaggerated the similarity of the goals of the engineer and employer and ignored the existence of legitimate differences. With disillusionment came the present-day attempt to bargain collectively and act as virile labor organizations, an attempt hardly more successful than the educational campaigns of old.

Professionalism and Personalities. The basic problem with the present-day attempt by many unions of engineers to bolster their program is the inability of members to resolve the question of the type of organization they want. The problem was sharply put in 1957 by Professor Benjamin Aaron who told a gathering of engineer-unionists their trouble was:

". . . you want to eat your cake and have it too; to gain all the benefits that stem from collective bargaining and unionism without engaging in the tactics of unionism; to wring concessions from management while at the same time remaining a part of management. You view the world in which you work and live not as it is but as the way it used to be, and probably never will be again. In short, you suffer from an acute ambivalence . . . a kind of schizophrenia. . . . So far, your inability to decide between these conflicting desires and values has reduced you to relative ineffectiveness. But you can't put off the resolution of this dilemma much longer. . . ."[8]

The "schizophrenia" Aaron refers to has its roots in the professional character and personality of the membership.

The professional attitude of the engineer toward his job makes him aware of problems in the entire field of professional practice rather than in only the immediate place of employment. Union members as engineers are concerned with the status of the profession as a whole and the opinions of the professional societies in particular. The personality of the union member is that of the average engineer, "a practical thinker who will approach a problem with facts rather than abstract mental processes or intangible human possibilities. . . . He is action-oriented, and is interested in accomplishments. . . . He is concerned with current problems and has an antipathy for intangible affairs and unlimited or seemingly endless problems. . . . He has respect for authority. . . . He desires smooth working relationships."[9]

As a result of these characteristics, the members of engineers' unions are divided into two camps: one champions the guild as a model for the organization and the other the labor union. As a guild, the organization would devote itself to the idea that engineers and managers have no real differences and management should have the final decision in any case. The guild would avoid contacts with other unions and would serve primarily as a link in the company's internal communication system. Most of those who see the union as a guild are members of unions that bar technicians and admit only professional engineers; they prefer elitism to the strength that accrues from large numbers. Their arguments benefit from the contract gains gratuitously supplied by tandem bargaining relationships with blue-collar locals in the same plants. Some of these unions also profit from the paternalism of employers with government contracts on a "cost-plus" basis. It was not until 1958 that one of the guild-oriented unions finally broke from tradition and struck over a conflict. Such an occurrence continues to be rare.

The engineers and technicians who prefer the labor union as a model for their organizations believe that differences between engineers and managers are unavoidable and legitimate. They believe the wisest resolution of these differences is arrived at through joint discussion and bargaining by relatively equal parties. The union of engineers modelled on a genuine labor union would seek mutual benefit in alliances with other unions, possibly even with the international unions, and would place alongside the company's internal communication system one of its own, one that would include a carefully managed grievance machinery. The supporters of this view are found in the single-firm unions that include technicians as well as engineers; they prefer the strength of numbers to the elitism of a few. Aware of and determined to resolve the "schizophrenia" Aaron spoke of in favor of orthodox union ways, the union supporters have backed nine strikes in the last 10 years. Such a display of militance may be even more common in the future if supporters of unionism for engineers have their way in the meeting hall, but not around the bargaining table.

Basic Characteristics. In their makeup, single-firm unions of engineers reflect compromises between proponents of the guild and of the labor union, as well as compromises between the professional character and personality of members and the demands of an employee organization. For example, the unions of engineers are not especially person-based. Rather, they incline to impersonal record-keeping, the careful transcription of all union matters, the wide dissemination of formal reports and bargaining data, and other extensive uses of the printed word. The unions prefer strategic rather than tactical approaches to a problem. They are not given to solving problems by persuasion or influence, but rather put the emphasis on facts and not feelings:

> "By his nature and in accordance with his training, the engineer firmly believes in the power of facts and logic.

Unions of Engineers

Often these logics conflict with the realities of economic life, and when they do the engineer cannot give way; he holds to the logics. Thus the engineering unions tend to substitute debate for give-and-take negotiations. . . . Related to the above characteristic is the engineer's lack of appreciation for the need for off-the-record discussions between negotiators in advance of contract negotiations."[10]

This characteristic formality is encouraged by the nature of white-collar work in large and impersonal factories, a typical setting for these independent unions.

Unions of engineers are not as shop-focused, and are rather more cosmopolitan in outlook than are independent unions of non-professional workers. As professionals the members encourage the attention of the union outside the company gates, and the professional field, rather than the immediate front office, is the focus. This concern with the field, however, does not prevent members from paying considerable attention to management. Many engineers plan on winning a promotion into supervisory or executive ranks. A common interest in promotion helps explain concern with the immediate employer and his various competitors.

Unions of engineers are basically conservative, although they are capable of occasional displays of considerable imagination. For example, during a rare strike, a union of engineers won valuable national headlines by distributing four thousand roses to women clerks crossing the picket line. The union explained that the roses were to emphasize its refusal to interfere with non-striking employees. The dynamism of this union is such that it has recently gone to considerable expense to revamp its constitution to permit organizing drives at other plants of the company. Such dynamism, however, is severely limited by the professional's traditional disdain for the ways of unions and by the engineer's middle-class orientation with its distrust of union political action and militancy. As a result, most unions prefer to solicit members rather than use a union-shop clause to compel membership. This conservative policy commits considerable, perhaps an excessive, amount of energy to frequent membership drives.[11] Similarly, the unions are so meticulously democratic that "union leaders who negotiate for the engineers are seldom in a position to speak authoritatively for the union."[12] The unions avoid political activities, community service programs, and social functions, thereby reflecting both the conservatism of members and the fact that most middle-class members have ties to political, service, and social groups outside the plants. The conservatism of members also helps explain their reluctance to process grievances. Engineers do not want to become personally involved; timidity combines here with a distaste for argument and a concern with future promotion. This reluctance hurts the union by minimizing its role and depriving it of a record useful in winning its goals in bargaining.

Finally, unions of engineers are led by their size and circumstance to modify the ideology of the independent union. The engineers do not share an ideological commitment to small organizations or censure of Government labor agencies, as the unions are frequently large organizations that deal with large concerns and they benefit considerably from Government protection against raiders from blue-collar unions. The ideology of the union of engineers stresses professionalism as a concern that outweighs all others. The ideology discourages vigor in labor-management relations, resentment against professional societies which regularly attack unions of engineers, and union participation in "strategic alliances" with international unions.

In sum, the union's basic characteristics serve to weaken the organizations. Unions of engineers are victims of a split personality. Neither completely guilds or labor unions, the organizations struggle uneasily between the two models, unable to resolve the crucial problem of organizational identity.

Union Leaders. Prominent among the men caught and hurt in the squeeze between guild and union supporters are the few willing to serve as leaders. They are predominantly drawn from two types of men: the socially aware individual for whom the union is a means of expression and self-help, and the aspiring leader for whom the union provides a means of exercising organizational and leadership skills and a means for attaining recognition.[13] These men, usually topflight engineers, profit from the experience of the permanent Executive Secretaries employed by several wealthy unions and from the considerable educational attainments of the membership. They are faced, however, with the necessity of meeting solid problems without the backing of a solid organization and suffer much as a result.

A measure of the extreme discomfort of executive posts (and of the engineer's orientation toward promotion) is available in the rapid turnover of union leadership. The organizations are sorely pressed by this problem: a former Executive Secretary of a 1,600 member union frankly notes:

> "One of our primary concerns is the matter of filling the leadership ranks. With only a single full-time paid officer, the Association relies on candidates stepping from the ranks each year to fill nine other posts on its Executive Board. The task of functioning full-time as an engineer and part-time in labor-management relations has been so demanding that very few have been willing to occupy an Executive Board post for more than one year.

> The constant ripple of movement from the bargaining unit into management draws in large numbers upon the [union] Council, the legislative and judicial body which sits as direct representatives of the general membership. Thus, this level of leadership has the same changing aspect as the Executive Board.

> The need for the leadership understanding the total aspect of labor relations is seldom fully met. The relatively brief exposure to such problems just does not permit more than a vague appreciation of the subject."[14]

While it is possible to argue that loss of union leaders to management ranks helps build a core of union sympathizers on "the other side of the fence," it is still a question whether the unions can survive such losses and persist to profit from such sympathy.

Professional Societies. One of the chief reasons for questioning the ability of the unions to survive is the unrelenting opposition of professional engineering societies. The leading

77

such organization, the fifty-thousand-member National Society of Professional Engineers, warns that unionization can harm engineers both as professionals and as individuals:

> "First, for engineers as individuals: There would be a classification of engineering positions, with minimum standards. Initiative would be discouraged, individual recognition stifled, opportunities limited, and advancement retarded. Personal prestige would be damaged and professional recognition diminished. A 'leveling' of salaries would result, and regimentation would follow.

> Second, for the engineering profession as a whole: The desire for higher intellectual attainments would be sacrificed to the concern for immediate advantages. The confidential relationships inherent in professional service would be lost in the hypocrisy of lip service. Stratification, fragmentation and splintering of the profession would continue."[15]

Unionism and professionalism, the NSPE concludes, are clearly incompatible.

As an alternative to unions, the Society supports employee associations known as "sounding-boards." These associations are designed to bring together all professional engineers in a single firm, managers as well as employees, to consider their mutual problems. This inclusion of managers in an employees' association is thought "desirable because without such integration at all levels of professional thinking, the profession loses its cohesive nature and the benefits of open interchange of ideas, opinions and comments."[16] Pioneered by General Electric, sounding-boards can now be found in sixteen locations, twelve at G. E. plants.[17]

There is some reason to doubt the foregoing arguments. Recent studies of the contracts and practices of unions of engineers by impartial academic investigators fail to find that salary differentials have been narrowed, that there is featherbedding, or that advancement has come to rest solely on seniority. Instead, the investigators have found that unions of engineers strengthen merit raise provisions, urge an increase in

78

the utilization of the professional's talents, and protect rate ranges. The unions also press for travel allowances, field bonuses, a voice in company patent policies, leave with pay to attend learned society meetings, and company allowances for society membership fees.[18]

There is also reason to question the legitimacy and effectiveness of the "sounding-board" as substitute for the union. The Supreme Court has recently held that such organizations are "labor organizations" particularly susceptible to domination by the employer.[19] NSPE insists that the Court's decision does not hold for all such organizations, but many companies have probably been frightened away from the boards. Critics, of course, have made much of the Court's decision and label the sounding-boards "company unions," "weak sisters," and "metaphysical debating societies."

Academic and legal findings to one side, the opposition of the professional societies to unions of engineers is undoubtedly a telling one. The professionalism of the union member encourages him to give serious attention to the pronouncements of the societies, and much of the character ambivalence of the unions can be traced to this criticism. Moreover, the unions themselves are reluctant to counterattack for fear of antagonizing their own members. On rare occasions, the unions have suggested in soft tones that the professional societies are too many in number, too conservative in character, and too amenable to the influence of employers.[20] The unions also make much of the fact that the law severely limits the bargaining activities that can be pursued by the societies. Overall, however, it is clear that the professional societies have helped check the expansion of the independent unions and have had a part in the recent collapse of several major unions of engineers.

Unions and Employers. In addition to their problems with the professional societies, the single-firm unions of engineers face considerable opposition from the management of the industries in which they are organized. Many companies have discovered the union's split personality and the resulting absence of power on the union's side. This knowledge has come to the companies at a particularly crucial point in union-management relations. The danger of unionization of engineers by international unions has been lessened by the Taft-Hartley Act, the McClellan Committee revelations, and the sagging strength of the major unions themselves. This has left companies free to re-evaluate the independent unions. Many companies now charge that the unions have had an adverse effect on employee morale. Some feel that the unions undercut the prestige of the supervisors and damage their morale. The tone of union publications is thought to discredit the company and weaken the engineer's loyalty to it. This in turn is held to hamper the company in competition, as in bidding on a government contract or in recruiting new talent. Other complaints by management center on the loss of unilateral control of incentives, the shift in bargaining power from first-line supervisors to the individual engineer, and the bother of being forced to specify decision criteria under union questioning. Above all these complaints, however, stands the matter of management's emotional reaction to the unions of their professional employees. Walton reports:

"Managers viewed the engineers as having been 'split off from management.' Unionization of professionals was regarded as a slap in the face—as one manager said, 'It doesn't hurt, it stings!' "[21]

Although a small number of managers think the unions encourage fair and alert management, and contribute to employee security, the largest number of managers appear firmly opposed to the unions of engineers.[22]

Employer opposition takes many forms. At its mildest, it may entail misrepresentation of the union's role:

"A majority of the management representatives made the general statement that the union had not improved the terms of employment for their engineers, or otherwise affected engineering operations. Yet, comments made in subsequent discussions with the same individuals about specific instances not infrequently led to the conclusion that the union *had* been instrumental in bringing about certain changes in policies and practices."[23]

Other more serious forms of opposition include the deliberate promotion of talented union officers into management ranks, the

strategic denial of information to the union, the constant misrepresentation of union policies, the denial of the courtesies or
the protocol common in union-management relations, and covert company support of the elements in the bargaining unit
that favor decertification of the union.

Inter-Union Relations. Single-firm unions of engineers have
been led to seek aid from other unions by the pressure of opposition from professional societies and employers. This opposition, in combination with the attention paid the field by
professionals, explains several attempts over the years to form
and maintain strong associations of similar unions. The most
recent and important of these attempts involves the now defunct Engineers and Scientists of America, an association
formed in 1952 by nine independent unions. The Association
was designed to provide hard-to-get facts on engineers, their
salaries, and their relations with management. It was also to
represent engineers before Congress, government agencies, and
the general public. Finally, it was to assist the attempt by professional employees to unionize unorganized plants.

Despite the seriousness of the needs that prompted its formation, the Association was hampered from the start by problems
common to all such associations, whatever the type of union or
member involved. Affiliates could not agree on what they
wanted from the association. There was considerable opposition from employers. The leaders of affiliates were never sure
of the support of their own members for the Association, and
were therefore reluctant to grant the Association enough authority for effectiveness. As if these problems were not enough,
the affiliates that refused membership to technicians remained
aloof from other unions that welcomed these quasi-professional
employees. Another serious rift divided those single-firm unions
that favored close relations with the international unions and
possibly even affiliation from those unions that preferred to
have no relations at all with the major unions. These rifts finally resulted in a showdown vote in 1956, in which those who
favored contact with the major unions lost the ballot.

Frustrated by the loss, several unions left the association.
These organizations, representing perhaps twelve thousand employees, have tried unsuccessfully ever since to form their own

association. The original Association has not fared any better. Tested in a decisive 1960 election at Western Electric, it proved weak, ineffective, and unpopular. An important affiliate, the Conference of Western Electric Technical Employees-National, was ousted by that company's 7,000 professionals. Shortly thereafter, in February, 1961, the Engineers and Scientists of America was disbanded.[24]

A few of the independent unions of engineers have recently begun to pay some attention to blue-collar international unions. Convinced that the associations are inadequate, and apprehensive of employer pressures, these independent unions are re-considering long-standing invitations to affiliate with major unions. For their part, faced with declining membership, the major unions are quite willing to make various concessions in order to win new members from among the increasing number of engineers in industry. Among others, the United Automobile Workers and the International Union of Electrical Workers have set up special organizing units and internal councils to handle the affairs of engineering and scientific personnel.[25] Paradoxically, however, these two international unions have been rejected in important recent votes on affiliation.[26] Walton notes in this connection that:

> "It is not clear just how interested those engineering union leaders who express an interest in affiliating with the shop union international really are. The threat to cooperate or affiliate with the shop union constitutes one of the most effective threats the engineers have to strengthen their own bargaining efforts. In effect they confront management with the following reasoning: A failure of the company to meet the needs of the members will convince these members of the necessity for stronger affiliations."[27]

This stratagem would probably be more effective if management were not so well aware of the union's failure to decide whether it wants to remain a weak union-like guild or become a strong guild-like union.

Unions of Engineers

The situation of single-firm independent unions of engineers is not an auspicious one. No major group has been added to the unionized ranks of engineers in eleven years and three large organizations have been disbanded by their members. At the heart of the union's plight is its failure to decide whether it is a guild or a labor union. As if this were not enough, the unions are a minority element in the relevant industries. They face indifference and even bitter opposition from non-members. They are seriously hurt when denied employer support. And their attempts at mutual aid regularly fail them. Until they resolve their own indecision about the nature of their organizations, single-firm independent unions of engineers face a rather bleak future.

FOOTNOTES

1. In contrast with the limited success of independent unions, note that the international unions have organized airline pilots, teachers, musicians, newspaper reporters, theater performers, technical engineers, and many others.

2. Data on the unions is taken from NSPE, *Tabulation of Unions Representing Engineering and Technical Employees* (Washington, D.C.: National Society of Professional Engineers, 1961). Possibly 40,000 of the nation's 650,000 engineers may be unionized in single-firm *and* multi-firm independent unions, and in the locals of certain international unions. Approximately 20,000 are actually dues-paying members, and fewer than 7,500 are in the international unions. "Engineering Union Fights for Life," *Fortune*, May, 1960, p. 246.

3. Note that the unions were after the blue-collar workers in industrial plants and were fairly casual about including or excluding the professional employees.

4. See the "professional provisions" of the Taft-Hartley Act: Sections 2 (12) and 9 (B) (1). A typical, if partial source is NSPE, *A Professional Look at the Engineer in Industry* (Washington, D.C.: National Society of Professional Employees, Engineer-in-Industry Committee, 1955).

5. McEachron, K. B., "Unionization of Professionals," *Journal of Engineering Education*, 44 (November, 1953), pp. 148-156.

6. Walton, Richard E., *The Impact of the Professional Engineering Union* (Boston, Mass.: Harvard University, 1961). Walton's study is the most thorough-going, balanced, and timely of all such reports; heavy reliance is placed on it throughout this chapter. Such use, however, is seriously compromised by Walton's failure to distinguish between single and multi-firm independent unions.

7. *Ibid.*, p. 25. Walton adds that while the relative importance of the educate-management approach "has declined somewhat over the years, it still is the unions' chief strategy." *Ibid.*, p. 37. See also Goldstein, Bernard, "The Perspective of Unionized Professionals," *Social Forces*, 37

Unions of Engineers

(May, 1959), pp. 323-327; Riegel, John W., *Collective Bargaining as Viewed by Unorganized Engineers and Scientists* (Ann Arbor, Michigan: Bureau of Industrial Relations, 1959).

8. Aaron, Benjamin, *Engineers and Scientists Guild Outlook*, July, 1957. Aaron, a university professor, delivered the warning at a banquet held by the ESG. This association, composed of mixed-union forces that favored pro-union acts, has since collapsed and disappeared.

9. Feree, Robert W., "Attitudes of Professional Engineers" (Unpublished MBA Thesis, University of Pennsylvania, 1960). See also Goldstein, Bernard, "Some Aspects of the Nature of Unionism Among Salaried Professionals in Industry," *American Sociological Review* (April, 1955), pp. 199-205.

10. Walton, *op. cit.*, p. 37. Walton adds that leaders who have appreciated a need for off-the-record discussions "have come in for severe criticisms from other engineers on the bargaining committee who do not think such talks are ethical." *Ibid.*, p. 38. This is a good example of the serious conflict between the engineer's intellectualized and idealized picture of the bargaining process and the hard realities of this process.

11. Reluctance to require membership means that the unions have fewer members than suggested by the number of employees represented. For example, nine single-firm unions of engineers have only 5,745 members even though the unions represent 9,500 engineers. This difference, in times of challenge, is often a fatal one. Here again organizational considerations are handicapped by personal tastes. See NSPE, *Tabulation . . . , op. cit.*

12. Walton, *op. cit.*, p. 38. The extravagant use of democratic forms slows down negotiations and thereby squanders interest and support. Also, by taking so much time and effort it effectively discourages new applicants for leadership positions. Management cites these so-called "delaying tactics" in explaining widespread opposition to the unions.

13. Walton, *op. cit.*, pp. 39, 40. Walton notes that the socially aware and leader aspirant types that provide leadership "are often a minority or only a small majority of the bargaining unit." *Ibid.*, p. 40. He adds that while "there was no correlation between the quality of an engineer and his activity or membership in a professional union" there were "indications that a larger than otherwise normal percentage of employees who have been union officers subsequently were promoted to managerial positions." *Ibid.*, pp. 39, 249.

14. Private correspondence, September 29, 1960. Over 100 of 150 former members of the Executive Council of this union are now in managerial positions. One union comments: "Most of our group leaders and managers were [union] men themselves—all are aware of its humanizing force. Few, indeed, are the leaders who criticize [the union's] aims and results as they also benefit from them." Anon., "Why Should RCA Engineers Join ASPEP?" *The Exponent*, October, 1961, p. 5.

15. Shoch, Clarence, "The Professional Union—A Contradiction," *Journal of Engineering Education*, Vol. 4, 1954, p. 354. See also any issue of *Engineering Employment Practices Newsletter*, published monthly in Washington, D.C., by the National Society of Professional Engineers. The professional societies are not alone in their outside opposition to unions of engineers; there is reason to suspect that the faculties of many engineering schools impress students with critical views of labor organizations.

16. Shoch, *op. cit.*, p. 349.

17. "Engineer Union Fights for Life," *Fortune, op. cit.*, p. 251.

18. Walton, *op. cit.* See also NICB, *Unionization Among American Engineers* (New York: National Industrial Conference Board, Studies in Personnel Policy, No. 155, 1956); Culley, Jack F., "A Primer on Engineering Unionism," *Iowa Business Digest*, November, 1958, pp. 10-14; Greenwood, David C., *The Engineering Profession and Unionization* (Washington, D.C.: Public Affairs Press, 1960).

19. See "Cabot Carbon Decision Stirs Interest re Sounding Boards," *Engineering Employment Practices Newsletter*, July, 1959, p. 2. Board supporters hope to clear up doubts with passage of a federal law that would explicitly exclude the Boards from the law's definition of labor organizations. *Ibid.*, pp. 3, 4. For the position of critics, see Amann, Joseph, "Collective Bargaining vs. Sounding Board," *APEP Exponent*, May-June, 1959, pp. 5, 6.

20. The unions get some support from the fact that many engineers show the same minimal interest in professional societies that most show in labor unions. The NSPE has attracted only 50,000 members from a potential at least ten times as large. Non-members, however, are probably aware of and may well approve of NSPE policies.

21. Walton, *op. cit.*, p. 369. Walton notes that "management's reaction to the engineering union is largely an emotional one, a reaction of an entirely different order from that which managers would exhibit if they were talking about a factor that merely encroached upon the ability of their companies to produce, or to sell, or to stay in business. They were talking about something that affected them personally, individually and collectively as managers," *ibid.*

22. Note, however, there is evidence management prefers single-firm unions of engineers to locals of the international unions. "The independents, they find, are more responsive to the wishes of the engineers they represent. And they are somewhat more reasonable in demands and grievances." Anon., "Are Professional Engineering Unions on the Way Out?" *Product Engineering*, August 29, 1960, p. 17. Walton suggests that employers "seem to be strictly opportunistic about the question of scope of unit . . . interested in achieving a unit that optimizes resistance to militant tendencies. . . ." Walton, *op. cit.*, p. 24.

23. Walton, *op. cit.*, p. 12. Walton adds that "the companies' official position on this question of impact is understandable. They do not want their respective unions to gain the reputation for being effective agents," *ibid.*

24. On ESA see "Engineer Union Fights for Life," *Fortune, op. cit.*; Walton, *op. cit.*, pp. 26, 27, 42-44; "Engineers Give Up 11-Year Drive to Form National Bargaining Unit," *Business Week*, February 18, 1961, p. 109. Discussion of the unsuccessful rival to ESA is available in most of the foregoing references, as well as in the *ESG Outlook*. Note that neither ESA nor its ill-starred rival were "pure" associations; both included multifirm, as well as single-firm independent unions (the distribution in both cases favored the latter type).

25. See Carey, James B., "Address," *Labor Looks at the White Collar Worker* (Washington, D.C.: AFL-CIO, 1957), pp. 21-28; Walton, *op. cit.*, pp. 44, 45.

26. See "UAW and ESA Ponder Honeywell Vote Significance," *Engineering Employment Practices Newsletter*, June, 1957, p. 1; "Sperry

Unions of Engineers

Engineers Follow Trend, Vote 'No Union,'" *Engineering Employment Practices Newsletter*, October, 1960, p. 1; "Unions Fear Bog-Down in Drive for Engineers," *Engineering Employment Practices Newsletter*, November, 1960. See also "Engineers Vote 'No Union' at Western Electric," *Engineering Employment Practices Newsletter*, June, 1960, p. 1.
    27. Walton, *op. cit.*, p. 44.

VIII. THE ASSOCIATIONS OF SINGLE-FIRM INDEPENDENT UNIONS

O NE of the more revealing paradoxes connected with single-firm independent unions is the desire of some to affiliate with other unaffiliated unions. They seek ties with others like them, and the associations that result could have a decisive influence on the future of the independent unions. Should the associations prosper, they would undoubtedly strengthen the affiliates. Should the associations falter, this might seriously weaken affiliates.

It should be clear from the outset that the associations are a minority phenomena. To judge from membership figures, the great majority of single-firm independent unions do not join associations.[1] Of the forty unions examined for this study (thirty-six blue-collar and four white-collar unions), only two were affiliates of a company-wide association, and only seventeen were members of an industry, state, or national association. Many unions do not join simply because they are totally unaware that such associations exist. Thirteen of the forty were this isolated.[2] Some do not believe the associations can do anything for them. Others do not want the problem of raising a per capita tax for the association. Still others fear affiliation would upset a pattern of harmonious employer-union relations. Typical of statements explaining strategic refusal to join an association was one offered by the head of a weak union of 52 dye company employees:

"We have nothing to do with other independents in the neighborhood or in other companies like ours. We don't pay any attention to the literature mailed us by the state or the national associations. It's in our by-laws, see, we have a bar against contacts with other independents. We wrote it in when we started up in 1956. We wanted to be strictly independent, and we felt the company might like the move and maybe give us a little more. . . ."

As a consequence of such sentiment, the large majority of association affiliates are strong independent unions, and this qualification immediately restricts the growth prospects of the associations.

Associations or loose federations of independent unions are a relatively recent development in the 60-year history of these unions. Shop committees and employee representation plans were not labor unions but rather tools of personnel administration, so neither showed any interest in federations.[3] The company union of the 1930's did show some interest and a few industry-wide associations were formed.[4] These groups were often handicapped by employee knowledge of employer support and by the lack of experienced leadership. Few of these groups survived their founding year and none persist today.[5] The contemporary association had its start during World War II when wage controls and other war regulations encouraged unions to look to state and federal agencies rather than to their immediate employers for contract gains.[6]

From 1941 to the present the nation's single-firm independent unions have sponsored four different types of association: the intra-company council, the industry-wide association, the state association, and the national association.[7] The form and accomplishments of each of the four are discussed below.

The Intra-Company Council. When the plants of a single company are organized by different unions, whether single-firm independents or local unions, the possibility exists that the employer's centralized labor relations policy will encourage cooperation among the various unions. Such cooperation is also common when only one type of union is involved, as in the case of both the UAW's Corporation Councils[8] and the Federation of Du Pont Independent Unions. Occasionally this cooperation is formalized, and an association of the employer's various unions is created. Affiliates expect the association to circulate contracts and to serve as a clearinghouse of data on the single employer and on other companies. Associations are expected to arrange demonstrations of support and collect material support for striking affiliates when necessary. The association in turn expects some funds from affiliates, reasonable cooperation, and ready support.

A representative explanation of interest in a "pure" council (one composed only of independent unions) was offered by the head of a weak union of 345 chemical company employees:

> "We are just plain sick and tired of the company paternalism. Sure, our contract is the best, but we want to bargain about more items and get fewer 'gifts.' . . . The Company Council may help us. We know the company industrial relations directors meet together; the man in our plant is always throwing system-wide data at us. So we like the idea of the independent unions in the system also getting together. Right now the company headquarters refuses to recognize the Council but we hope this will change . . . we are not going to join the State Association until we first make a success of our own organization."

Other presidents voiced equal commitment to their company councils.[9]

Typical of the "pure" company association is the Federation of Westinghouse Independent Salaried Unions. This organization included the white-collar workers at thirty separate Westinghouse locations. The Federation is unique for its active intracompany organizing campaign, its successful integration of engineers and clerical workers, and its strained labor relations.[10] Another group, composed of Du Pont independent union members, has a less successful record. Company opposition in this instance helped limit association membership, morale, and accomplishments.[11]

Somewhat more common is the company council that includes both independent unions and local unions of the international labor organizations. These differ from any others discussed in this chapter by reason of their "impure" character. Their mixed nature means that the independent is exposed at first hand to the relatively greater resources, financial, intellectual, and political, of the international union. This exposure may constitute a ceaseless, subtle pressure to affiliate with the international. An example of this was provided by the leader of a union of 80 utility company employees who recalled:

> "We used to have a working agreement of all the gas plant unions in the company. I helped set it up and it

worked pretty good for a time. In a while though it fell apart. Some lawyer connected with one of the larger independent unions got the bright idea that we should all form one union to deal with the company. None of us liked one another enough for that so soon the whole thing broke up. No merger, no working agreement, nothing."

The president of a strong union of 450 filter company employees rejected overtures for the formation of a company council when he sensed affiliation pressures:

"There are nine plants in this chain and we are the largest. Our union is the only independent. The other unions in other plants would like company-wide bargaining, but they are not trustworthy. I do not call them, they call me. A few of them tried to set it up but we reserved judgment. They were fishy guys out fishing, always fishing. In the back of their minds was affiliation. We sensed it and want no part of it or them."

For other independent unions the fact of membership in a mixed association entails a gentlemen's pact with the local unions not to discuss affiliation, this pact often providing the independent with more security than that available under other common circumstances.[12]

In terms of association rewards, the president of 2,000-member union of toilet-goods company employees reported:

"All of the unions in the company's different plants meet together, regardless of affiliation. We exchange ideas, contracts, gossip, and that sort of stuff. Why, we even sit in on one another's negotiations. I'll be going out to Kansas City this year to help the union out there look strong at the bargaining table. The guys out there will come East and help me when my time comes. In 1955 we showed the company we meant business. Three of us struck at one time and tied them up across the country. . . . This is the way all independent unions will go; this is the way of the future."

Similarly, the president of a 58-man union of oil truck drivers noted:

Associations

"The company wants to bargain for all its refineries and depots on the East Coast. We don't mind because wages in petroleum are an industry matter, so we meet in a ten-union council. . . . We prepare three months for negotiations and we give them a stiff fight . . . my members like the Council because it makes them feel we ain't a company union, and they remember when we almost struck two years ago, all the Council guys came in a big car caravan to help us out."

Such substantial returns on membership help explain interest in this particular form of association.[13]

The Industry-wide Association. There are only two industries with industry-wide associations of independent unions: the telephone and petroleum industries. The presence of associations in these particular industries has several explanations: The independent unions in telephones and petroleum have had a long and relatively successful history. The companies involved are directly related or closely follow one another's labor policies. In recent years able international unions in the industries have intensified competition with the independent unions. Associations profit from the concern of their affiliates with the threat of raids. This concern brings experienced leadership from established independents into the service of the association.[14]

The telephone industry associations have been considered in Chapter 6, and discussion, accordingly, is confined here to the type of blue-collar association found in the petroleum industry. A representative association known as the Federation of Independent Oil Unions (FIOU) was formed in 1955.[15] This followed an unsuccessful attempt by international unions the previous year to form one big organization of all petroleum unions, independents *and* locals. The attempt was too ambitious; the various unions had a long history of rivalry, and many independents feared the costs of a merger would force them to increase dues. They chose instead to pull closer together and the FIOU, rather than the visionary One Big Union, was the outcome. The Federation was designed to distribute information and to provide protection from raids expected from international unions after the 1955 AFL-CIO merger. By

Associations

1958 the Federation had grown to represent about 20,000 members in six independent unions.

At present the Federation does not have an easy time. Petroleum companies do not welcome its existence; its six affiliates are located in three different states; and the affiliates do not always pay the per capita contributions they pledge. A further and most serious problem is the inability of the Federation to discipline affiliates. The Federation was powerless in 1959, for example, when "turncoat" leaders of its largest affiliate (about 4,000 members) decided to discontinue their payment of ten cents per capita in order to discredit independents in general and boost chances for affiliation with an international union in a pending election. Significantly, the election outcome, a sharp repudiation of affiliation and a strong endorsement of the independent union had the effect of strengthening the Federation. Its largest member union was securely back in the fold by 1960 at the same time that the intensity of the contest and the disappearance of another affiliate that lost a raid in 1959 demonstrated to other petroleum unions the need for "strength in unity."

The advantages of membership in the industry-wide associations are the same as those possible from other types, with one major addition. Unlike the other types of association, the industry-wide group is in direct competition with international unions in the area. The fact that the associations are a direct counterpart to some international unions serves to dull the arguments of many ambitious independent union members who favor affiliation with an international union. For this reason, the stakes associated with federation success are highest here of any such situation and association shortcomings or failure the most portentous.

The State Association. The weakest of the four types of multiunion association is probably the state-wide association. There are only four operating, and all but one of these are sponsored by a national association of independent unions.[16] The weakness of these associations is largely due to their two-part *raison d'etre*; concern with state affairs and protection from international union raiders. State affairs do not excite popular interest, or at least enough to stir grass-roots support for affiliation with a statewide association of independent unions. And the fact of common presence in a single state is not an especially strong bond among unions of different size, industrial character, and location. The bond does not sustain any meaningful inter-union aid. In contrast, company and industry-wide associations offer a bread-and-butter focus of understandable interest. The national associations offer large size, wide scope of operations, lofty goals, and the like. The state-wide associations offer little in comparison and this tells in their record.

A representative association studied by the writer has forty affiliates with a total of 5,000 members from among the state's one hundred or so single-firm unions.[17] The association pledges in its constitution to coordinate independent union activities throughout the state, to disseminate information, to engage in legislative activities, and "to do all things which may be necessary or proper to secure for the workers the enjoyment of their natural rights." In order to implement these objects, it undertakes five major functions: it provides a central point for contacts, and supports bargaining, legislative, political, and educational activities.

As a central point for contacts, the association introduces union presidents to one another and encourages these men to exchange collective bargaining and other valuable information. One result of such contact was a recent and unprecedented survey of the wages and fringes prevailing at twelve independent organized establishments. In addition to this wage survey and other information exchanges, the association aids member unions in their bargaining activities by offering the services of its labor lawyer, certified public accountant, and time study expert. It also intervenes on request to help break deadlocks. Furthermore, the organization backs contract demands with a promise of adequate strike aid. Similar aid is available to member unions challenged by AFL-CIO unions seeking a representation election.

The association's political action program centers about its legislative resolutions, its state capital activities, and its publicity and publication efforts. Resolutions passed at the 1960 Convention called for a raise in the maximum payments under unemployment compensation, the establishment of a State Labor Relations Board, a raise in temporary disability benefits, more adequate state aid to local education, and sixteen other proposals. Regular visits are made to state legislators to aid in the implementation of these proposals. These visits purportedly help the association gain some recognition from state agencies and a degree of representation in state affairs proportionate to that afforded the state CIO and AFL.

Publications are employed to help keep readers aware of the association's political program and of new legal developments that might affect constituent unions or their members. A permanent and fulltime secretary is especially important to this aspect of the overall program. Finally, the association supports the infrequent educational activities of member unions by providing mimeographed and staff assistance, research resources, and personal contacts with noted educators. It sponsors seminars for affiliates on time study techniques, the Landrum-Griffin Act, defenses against AFL-CIO raids, grievance procedure, and other subjects.

This state association, then, is certainly not without its accomplishments. For example, an officer boasted:

"... we helped settle a short strike just a little while ago. We managed to get fifteen dollars to the strikers the first week and ten dollars the second. . . . The Governor and his wife held a reception after the elections. We went to the State Mansion and they thanked us. . . . Independent unions are beginning to get recognition in this state. The Commissioner of Labor knows we exist, the agencies know we exist. . . ."

The state association, in short, has an impressive record of activities—despite its inability to excite a majority of the state's independent unions about state affairs and its inability to wield its affiliates into a rewarding whole.

National Association. The National Association of Independent Unions* has 300 affiliates with possibly 75,000 members in a dozen or more states.[18] The larger of the country's two such outfits, it promises affiliates the benefits offered by state organizations with some important differences.[19] First, the scope

---

* Name chosen by author to preserve the association's anonymity.

of operations is greater; and second, the focus of the Association is on Washington, D.C., rather than on a state capital. The Association boasts that it is a "national organization that is recognized in Washington, and throughout the country, as an official voice for Independent Unions." It offers affiliates a four-page labor newspaper, a magazine of labor events, and the opportunity to attend meetings of regional and industry councils, an annual Washington political seminar, and an annual convention. Like the state associations, it also provides bargaining information and lends negotiators to bargaining affiliates. It represents independent unions before governmental committees and agencies, and helps coordinate the activities of affiliates.

Much of the Association's limited resources go into time-honored campaigns to secure new recognition for independent unions from federal government agencies, to gain their addition to the Bureau of Labor Statistics' *Directory of Labor Unions*, and to earn the sympathy of noted legislators for them. A major concern is the establishment of a Congressional Committee on independent unions similar to the Senate and House Labor Committees.[20] The Association wants a separate committee for independents because it feels pro-AFL-CIO congressmen dominate the present congressional committees. Similarly, the Association resents the fact that the Labor Advisory Committee of the Department of Labor is composed of "two gentlemen who represent the large Federation."[21]

The Association is not without its accomplishments. For example, the president of a weak union of 200 electrical company employees had this to say about it:

"We are one of the oldest members in the Association, joined in 1952, we did. And a good thing, too. Like when we struck for five weeks in 1960 we got considerable help from the Association and some of the members. We had no provision for strike benefits but we did manage to give $400 or $500 in relief. The Association circulated a letter in our behalf and member unions in St. Louis, Chicago, New Jersey, Pennsylvania, New York, and even two or three in California sent us money and letters of encouragement.

Associations

We returned the money with our warm appreciation . . . everybody knows they can also count on us if they need dollars or support. We sent $300 to a sister union down the road just a few months ago. Why, the boys in the shop would like to send even more than we do."

The same leader also valued the Association's ability to protect its reputation and that of all affiliates, at the same time that it rectified what could be a common shortcoming in association admittance policies:

"We were pretty upset when the newspapers linked us to the upstate shooting of that union organizer. The poor guy had been a member of one of eleven small unions run by a New York City family group. I was called to Washington, D.C., for a meeting on the whole problem, and within five days we had thrown all eleven unions the hell out of our outfit. The kingpin brought a battery of lawyers to plead for him, like arguing he had not broken any law and his organizer was a martyr not a hoodlum or goon. We heard him out, and then voted him out. After all, we got to think of our reputations. . . ."

When asked how the family group had won admission into the Association in the first place, the respondent answered that the names of applicants were circulated for approval prior to admission; "but after all, you can't expect small men like me to know every labor racketeer in business."

Other Association accomplishments include a mailing list of "approximately 2,500" single-firm independent unions, testimony at hearings on Taft-Hartley amendments and the public support for independents occasionally offered by the members of the House of Representatives. Above all, there is the confidence of affiliates that theirs is a sound and promising organization. The president of a strong union of 650 chemical company employees noted:

"We used to be in the State Association but the day we heard about this outfit we dropped the state boys and went national. In fact, we keep pushing the officers of the State Association to bring the whole bunch into the National. The cost is the same for us, but you get more service and you get national recognition. We'd like the National to put on a full-time officer and we hope some delegate from our union wins a big post with the association. What I mean is, we will never affiliate with an international union so long as we can bank on the National."

Whether such sentiment reflects considered judgment, or an act of faith, or possibly even one of desperation remains to be established. Whatever the explanation, the Association understandably welcomes such support.

Problems. Associations confront many and diverse problems. This was made clear by the recollections of a delegate to a national association's 1960 convention:

"They told me they had several hundred affiliates but there weren't more than fifty unions represented, if that much. . . . The delegates from big unions tried to lord it over guys like me from smaller groups. We got into a very bitter floor fight over a dues increase for the Association. The small guys finally held it down to a compromise ten per cent increase. Hell, we can't talk the same kind of dollars the big boys do. . . . A lot of our problems came from the fact that delegates couldn't stay for all the discussion and votes. Their unions couldn't afford but one day in convention expenses or the boss refused to give them more time off. This really hurt our caucus of small union delegates. . . . Yeh, we got some newspapers publicity. I'd have been damn well pleased though if we didn't. The crumby local newspaper in [convention city] identified us as locals of AFL-CIO unions. We think the newspaper guys did it deliberately because they were AFL-CIO members."

Systematically put, the problems posed by single-firm unaffiliated unions which join associations but behave as if they had not are essentially five: Company and industry councils frequently encounter employer opposition; affiliate leaders cannot always deliver the support of members; the situation of an affiliate is not always supported by the characteristics or actions of the association; the affiliates decline to tax themselves to provide adequate association resources; and the affiliates refuse to grant the associations the authority necessary for effectively coordinated action.

Company-wide and industry councils of independent unions for independents and local unions frequently run into employer opposition. Where employers have a bargaining advantage that accrues from the fragmentation of worker organization, employers seldom welcome loss of the advantage. In the chemical industry, for example, where a majority of unionized workers are in independent unions:

> ". . . the major chemical firms have revealed an unbending resistance to dealing with unions on anything other than a local basis. Some companies, particularly American Cyanamid and Monsanto, have resorted to a modified form of Boulwareism to thwart the development of multiplant bargaining on matters like wages, vacations, and holiday pay. Here, management has offered to negotiate contract extensions providing for attractive wage increases which would take effect before the existing contract is scheduled to expire. Acceptance of this offer by individual locals has then precluded them from taking joint action with other locals."[22]

Even after councils are formed, employer opposition is noted. For example, in Congressional testimony given in 1954 the head of a now defunct petroleum industry council of independents and local unions vigorously maintained that industry leaders intent on destroying the council had taken several disturbing moves in that direction.[23] This sort of testimony was repeated to the writer in 1960-1962 by representatives of other associations that bargained directly with employers (i.e., all but state and national associations).

A particularly serious problem of all associations of single-firm independent unions is the frequent inability of affiliate leaders to win the support of members for the association. The president of a weak union of 58 oil depot workers offered a typical report:

Associations

"The state association is a good thing. It is long overdue and should help hold us independents together. I only wish I could get this across to the boys. They refuse to pay the dues asked by the association and they think the annual convention is a booze and dame excursion. We get information free from other independents but I still think we could use the association. I just can't get the others thinking this way."

Similarly, the president of a strong union of 60 paint company employees told the writer:

"We joined the State Association six years ago after I campaigned for three years to get enough votes. I told the boys that being an independent alone left you in the dark while the Association would help us by being a clearinghouse for information. They bought my argument and everything was okay until three years ago when one of the oldsters carried stories back from an Association Convention. He bragged about how drunk he got and stuff like that. So now I can't get no support for the Association. The boys have small pocketbooks and small minds. Two years now they have voted down a measly appropriation to send delegates to the convention. . . . It's a damn shame but it's their money."

In this and other ways the conservatism of members impedes the relations of affiliates with associations.

A third problem arises from frequent conflict between the situation of an affiliate and some concern of the association. For example, the president of a strong union of 38 oil depot employees complained:

"I meet other independent union leaders in our industry four times a year in Philadelphia. We have a sort of information exchange. The problem is that most of the guys represent refineries and have big worries about automation. My boys are in sales, so we don't have no worry with automation. We got different problems. So sometimes other union leaders bore them. . . . Sales has no industry association of its own because the sales shops are too small. They couldn't afford sending delegates to a meeting. So I stick with the refinery group, though sometimes I wonder why."

An association move that angered affiliates was reported by a former association member, the president of a weak union of 450 filter company employees:

"We used to have contacts with other independents through the State Association. We quit. They got us angry with their special newspaper edition on the Landrum-Griffin. We knew the law required us to distribute a copy to all the guys so we appreciated it when the Association offered us the Law printed in its paper. But when we read the issue we hit the roof. They packed a lot of politics in along with the Law and also took a slap or two at the bosses. We couldn't distribute it in our shop, not without stirring a hornet's nest. So we pulled it out and we pulled out. We hear the Association had to withdraw copies from other shops for the same reason."

Another sort of action that often alienates or even loses members is the association's behavior in difficult bargaining situations. The association's problem is that it does not get a call for aid until a bargaining situation has reached an impasse. The association can then offer little real aid, especially as its strike-relief funds are very limited. Affiliates do not always understand this, as was evident in the comments of a disillusioned leader of 65 mill workers:

"We joined the state association in 1954, though to this day I don't know why. We always get a weak contract, the association don't help no how. Last time we asked for fifteen cents increase in a one-year contract. When the talks bogged down we sent for association officers. They sold us on six cents the first year and six cents more the second year in a two-year deal. The association guys seemed too friendly with the boss, and were always saying how tough a company it was to negotiate with. Hell, that's why we sent for them. . . . There is some sentiment to leave the association. It seems a little shady to us."

Associations

Whatever the facts in this specific situation, it provides a good illustration of the sort of problem associations find it difficult to avoid.

As a result of disappointment or as a reflection of a low level of expectations, affiliates decline to tax themselves to provide adequate association resources. None of the associations have the treasuries their officers think necessary. A regular feature at association conventions is a floor fight over an increase in the association's per capita tax, a fight usually settled by a compromise that leaves no one satisfied. This lack of funds means the associations cannot afford top legal, accounting, or time study specialists nor can they provide meaningful strike aid. Funds are not the only resource the affiliates deny associations. The affiliates also decline to conduct vital grass-roots programs such as campaigns in support of association-endorsed politicians, without which the association is powerless.

Finally, the many single-firm independent unions that join associations but behave as if they had not are responsible for a serious problem concerning association authority and affiliate autonomy. The association founders and officers desire the authority to speak for affiliated unions and to commit them to advisable political, social, and economic programs. Supporters of a strong association ask affiliates to pledge membership for several years, raise association dues, and allow centralized programs. Most affiliates, however, are jealous of their autonomy and are committed to the independence, self-government, and self-sufficiency basic to the single-firm independent union. These affiliates generally refuse to commit themselves to an association for more than a year or two. They fight attempts to raise dues and resist moves that would augment their dependency on the association, such as the establishment of a central strike fund.[24]

The problem here is basically one of definition: Those who are committed to the associations think of them as something above and apart from the affiliated unions. They support programs designed to build the associations even at the cost of the rugged independence of affiliates.[25] Those who are primarily committed to the unions themselves conceive of the associations as a staff adjunct of constituent unions; the associations are not expected to exist for themselves. Affiliates of this persuasion recognize that they have compromised their autonomy by joining associations and they resolve to resist any further loss. These rival camps of association boosters and affiliate boosters turn pertinent gatherings into struggles serious enough to cast doubt on the association's proper form and on the likelihood of its continued existence.

These five problems are not unique to the associations of independent unions. Rather, in one degree or another they are common to all combinations of labor organizations (such as city and state labor councils of local unions, the international unions, and the AFL-CIO). There are two major differences, however, that intensify the dilemma of the associations of independent unions. For one, the five problems are greater where independents are involved. Their associations are more vulnerable to employer opposition, leaders have less control over members, the affiliates are more diverse and less sophisticated, the affiliates are poorer and are less inclined to raise necessary revenue, and the affiliates are more deeply committed to autonomy than even the most independent-minded of local unions. Secondly, the source of the problems in the associations of independents can be traced to the basic "personality" characteristics of the affiliates. An association of local unions entails a basic commitment of affiliates to "strength in unity" and other principles of centralization. An association of single-firm independent unions is compelled by the basic nature of its affiliates to skirt such a commitment. This crucial difference means the five association problems might be remedied by associations of local unions, but might never be adequately handled in a framework of associations of independents.

In what ways are the basic problems of the associations due to the characteristics of affiliates? Single-firm independent unions are basically plant-oriented and employer-centered. Their first and foremost concern is with events of the immediate work-place. While it is true that the strong unions attracted by the associations modifies these basic traits and are distinguished for their extra-plant orientation, it is also true that the leaders recognize and honor the narrow shop-focus of most members. The unions are also "person-based." Many are there-

Associations

fore wary of the staff assistance offered by the associations and reject the procedural route of the association in favor of their own personal touch in labor-management relations. Finally, the unions are conservative organizations with an ideological commitment that elevates smallness to a positive virtue. Many affiliates therefore reject association plans for expansion and large-scale projects as ultra-progressive and accept slow association growth as right and proper whatever its limits on association effectiveness. Many unions refuse to surrender precious grants of autonomy or recognize the interests of the associations. Their ideology values self-rule above all else, including effectiveness.[26]

The limited performance of the associations has its roots in the character of affiliates, weaknesses therein magnified many times by the lens of association. The basic "personality" characteristics conflict with the need in a cooperative effort for great resources, central authority, and sacrifice from affiliates. As a result, the record of most associations is one of disappointed hopes, frustrated plans, and unrealized goals, traceable in largest part to association affiliates themselves. The associations may yet play a decisive role in promoting the viability of the independent unions, or their collapse. They may yet wield isolated independents into a loose, but rewarding "movement." At present, however, they are inconspicuous victims of the indifference of outsiders, their failure to attract new affiliates, and the inadequacies of ambivalent insiders.

FOOTNOTES

1. The leading state association and the leading national association have possibly 375 affiliates between them. Moreover, many independent unions have memberships in two or more associations. For corroborative data, see Bureau of Labor Statistics, *Membership Survey of Intrastate Unions and Single-Employer Unions in the United States, 1961* (Washington, D.C.: BLS, Department of Labor, 1962. In preparation).

2. Lack of knowledge of the associations can be explained by the semi-rural location of isolated small unions, the lack of inter-union ties,

Associations

and the absence of mass media discussion of the associations. Efforts to change the situation (e.g., extensive use of free mailings) have met with limited success.

3. Interest in associations was effectively discouraged by employers anxious to quarantine militant employees in other plants and to restrict the resources of employees to those available in the immediate workplace.

4. As many of the company unions of the 1930's were employer-dominated, it is probably correct to assume that the new interest in associations reflected a change in employer evaluation of the phenomena. In the late 1930's the goal of many employers switched from domination alone to protecting the bare survival of single-firm independent unions pressed both by the new NLRB and reinvigorated international unions; the first associations appeared in industries marked by the greatest employer meddling in union affairs.

5. Like present-day associations, the early organizations were staffed by part-time officers already burdened with the affairs of their own unions. Similarly, affiliates refused necessary funds or authority. Unlike most present-day associations the early organizations were especially handicapped by apparent employer meddling in association affairs.

6. Single-firm unions look to Washington, D.C., not only for wage gains but also for fair treatment. A concern that Federal boards would give more to local unions than to the independent is considered a major explanation of interest at the time in associations. Edelman notes that "unions not affiliated with the CIO or AFL were . . . at an observable disadvantage in World War II; during the Korean War these were accorded a measure of formal representation." A positive correlation between association growth and the centralization of industrial relations decision-making in Washington, D.C., is evident over the last 20 years. Edelman, Murray, "Interest Representation and Policy Choice in Labor Law Administration," *Labor Law Journal,* March, 1958, p. 221.

7. A fifth type of association, one confined to unions of engineers, is considered in Chapter 7.

8. A typical Corporation Council includes representatives from the widely scattered UAW locals of the General Motors Company. Other examples include the General Electric Conference Board of the IUE and the system boards of the railroad unions. "The purpose is to bring to bear authority comparable in scope to the scope of the labor market drawn on by the employer or the product market scope of the employer's operations." Barbash, Jack, *Labor's Grass Roots: A Study of the Local Union* (New York: Harper & Brothers, 1961) p. 135.

9. A 1955 study of 13 international union locals and three independent unions located in New Jersey found a "strong preference for company-wide rather than single-plant negotiations . . . it strengthens the unions' main economic weapon, . . . it facilitates the achievement of uniform wages and working conditions, and . . . management decision-making on such matters is centralized." France, Robert R., *Union Decisions in Collective Bargaining* (Princeton, N.J.: Industrial Relations Section, Princeton University, Report Series No. 90, 1955) p. 10.

10. Among other Federation claims, a former president notes that: "Due to being unorganized, the poor white-collar worker had no one to represent him in Washington . . . , consequently, his problems did not receive the consideration which they so justly deserve until the officers

Associations

of the Federation . . . , duly authorized spokesmen for their organization and self-appointed spokesmen for the unorganized white-collar employees throughout the country, appeared in Washington. . . ." Bollens, Leo F., *White Collar or Noose? The Occupation of Millions* (New York: North River Press, 1947) p. 205. See also Federation of Westinghouse Independent Salaried Unions, *It Pays to be a Union Member* (Pittsburgh, Pa.: FWISU, 1947); Federation of Westinghouse Independent Salaried Unions, *The Regulator*, 1946 to date.

11. "Loose federations of independent unions have been established in Du Pont and Procter & Gamble but neither of these councils exercises any authority over its affiliates. . . . In the Du Pont chain, management has held to a policy of negotiating all issues on a local basis, notwithstanding the fact that its comprehensive—and generous—program of fringe benefits is formulated at the headquarters level . . . the major chemical firms have revealed an unbending resistance to dealing with unions on anything other than a local basis." Weber, Arnold R., "Competitive Unionism in the Chemical Industry," *Industrial and Labor Relations Review*, October, 1959, pp. 19, 34. Additional information was obtained in interviews with officers of three independent unions of Du Pont employees.

12. Local union participation with independent unions in company councils is part of a newly emerging pattern of inter-union relations, a pattern that emphasizes wooing instead of raiding the independent unions. See Chapter 9, "Relations with the Internationals: Competition and Cooperation." See also "Esso Conference in Washington," *The International Teamster*, April, 1959, pp. 7-8.

13. Evidence of the popularity of company-wide associations is available in the pending strengthening of one and the pending formation of a new association. See "Standard Independents Show Further Crack-Up," *OCAW Union News*, April 27, 1959, p. 3; "Humble Oil Independent Unions Plan Federation," *IRC Current News*, December 21, 1961, p. 237; "New Name in CPI's Labor Line-Up," *Chemical Week*, February 3, 1962, pp. 45-46.

14. While strong today in telephones and petroleum, the associations have dramatically failed in years past in utilities and telephones. The United Utilities Union, which in 1942 included 30 independent unions and represented over 250,000 members, has long since been absorbed by the AFL-CIO Utility Workers Union. The National Federation of Telephone Workers, which grew in the 1940's to include almost 50 independent unions, has since become the Communications Workers of America, AFL-CIO. On the NFTW, see Chapter 6, "Unions of White-Collar Workers." See also Barbash, Jack, *Unions and Telephones: The Story of the Communication Workers of America* (New York: Harper & Brothers, 1952). On the United Utilities Union, see "Utility Union Formed," *The CIO News*, April 15, 1946, p. 7.

15. This discussion of the Federation of Independent Oil Unions relies heavily on Marshall, F. Ray, "Independent Unions in the Gulf Coast Petroleum Refining Industry," *Labor Law Journal*, September, 1961, pp. 823-840. Information on other associations in the petroleum industry is extremely rare.

16. The National Independent Union Council has chartered state associations in California, Kansas, Michigan, Pennsylvania, Iowa, and

Associations

Missouri. The writer, however, has reason to question whether all six associations are operative. The one state association operating outside of the NIUC is the Independent Unions of New Jersey. For details on NIUC state affiliates, see Bureau of Labor Statistics, *Directory of National and International Labor Unions in the United States, 1961* (Washington, D.C.: U.S. Department of Labor, 1962).

17. The association claims over 100 affiliates with a total membership of 25,000 workers.

18. The association claims 1,000 affiliates with a total of 1,800,000 members. It also claims to speak for fifty million workers (those outside of international unions) although it cannot cite any concrete delegation of authority from these non-unionists. Interestingly, a high official in the AFL-CIO Department of Organization has credited the Association with 150,000 to 200,000 members. Private correspondence, November 25, 1958.

19. The nation's other national association has declined considerably since its formation in 1942. While the founders claimed a million members and *Business Week* predicted a future membership of 300,000, the Association never prospered. At present it has about 40 affiliates and possibly 45,000 members. On current figures for this association see Thompson, Kenneth M., *Labor Unions in Louisiana* (Baton Rouge, La.: Louisiana State University, 1959), p. 45. The Association in 1954 claimed to represent over 2,000,000 members. U.S. Congress, Senate, Committee on Labor and Public Welfare, *Hearings, Taft-Hartley Act Revisions*, 83rd Congress, 1st Session, Part 2, 1953, p. 678. Note that the two national associations have failed in recent merger attempts. See *New York Times*, December 19, 1955; Philip Taft, "Independent Unions and the Merger," *Industrial and Labor Relations Review*, 9 (April, 1956), p. 446; *Trade Union Courier*, April 10, 1959. In 1956 *Fortune* suggested that neither association would prosper until both merged. "Independents Begin to Huddle," *Fortune*, March, 1956, pp. 203-206.

20. House Resolution No. 188 introduced by Representative Cunningham of Iowa and House Resolution No. 129 introduced by Representative Hiestand of California both supported the establishment of a Committee on Independent Unions. *The Labor Journal*, April 15, 1957, p. 1. Troy suggests that "the chief activity of the independents' federations . . . has been lobbying before Congress and state legislatures." Troy, Leo, "Local Independent Unions and the American Labor Movement," *Industrial and Labor Relations Review*, 14 (April, 1961), p. 344.

21. *The Labor Journal*, April 4, 1958. Note that this suspicion of AFL-CIO influence over the Department of Labor is the Association counterpart of the suspicion common to individual independents. See the discussion of ideology in Chapter 2, "Personality of the Union: An Overview."

22. Weber, *op. cit.* See also Barbash, Jack, *Unions and Telephones, op. cit.*; France, Robert R., *Union Decisions in Collective Bargaining, op. cit.*

23. In 1954, a union leader testified that a coalition of union forces in the petroleum industry was vigorously opposed by management forces that preferred isolated collective bargaining units. "They want this even though they have a 'coalition' of their own, through the American Petroleum Institute, through interlocking directorates of so-called competing

companies, through joint ownership of subsidiary operating companies, and through integrated products pipeline system." U.S. Congress, Senate, Committee on Labor and Public Welfare, *Hearings, Taft-Hartley Act Revisions,* 83rd Congress, 1st Session, Part 3, 1953, p. 1644. For an account of a similar situation involving an association in the telephone industry, see U.S. Congress, Senate, Subcommittee on Labor-Management Relations, *Hearings, Labor-Management Relations in the Bell Telephone System,* 81st Congress, 2nd Session, 1953, p. 56.

24. Troy notes in this connection that "unlike the AFL-CIO and its predecessor federations of labor, the associations of local independent unions do not have the function of 'validating' affiliates' jurisdictional claims. . . . Each union claims jurisdiction only over the workers in a single plant, not over the whole industry or class of workers. Consequently, the independent federations have even less control over affiliates than the AFL-CIO." Troy, Leo, *op. cit.,* p. 344.

25. The writer is inclined to disagree with Troy when he writes: "Despite their small numbers, the federations have imparted to the local independent union the definite character of a movement. They constitute centers about which the growing numbers of local independents can cluster." Troy, Leo, "Local Independent and National Unions: Competitive Labor Organizations," *The Journal of Political Economy,* LXVIII (October, 1960), p. 504.

26. According to Taft, an association, "unless aided by substantial secessions from the merged federation, is likely to be an anemic organism, which will give to its affiliates few of the advantages of belonging to a larger federated body." Taft, Philip, "Independent Unions and the Merger," *Industrial and Labor Relations Review,* 9 (April, 1956), p. 434. In 1958 a graduate student at the University of Maryland surveyed 46 officers of 16 AFL-CIO unions concerning associations. Seventeen had never heard of the associations, thirty-eight denied the associations had made any contributions to collective bargaining, and forty-six doubted that independent unions would eventually form one united association or that present associations were a threat to AFL-CIO power. Lukow, Neil B., "A Current Study of Independent Unions in the United States" (Unpublished Master's Thesis, University of Maryland, 1959). The writer obtained similar results from a 1961 survey of the staff officers of twenty international unions. The writer also found a striking lack of concern with the associations on the part of company representatives interviewed in 1961-1962.

IX. RELATIONS WITH THE INTERNATIONALS: COMPETITION AND COOPERATION

Previous chapters have suggested that the independent single-firm union, strong or weak, blue-collar or white-collar, generally does not match the resources, gains, and initiative of the major international unions. Moreover, independents acting in concert via associations are still no match for even small internationals. How, then, have the single-firm unions managed to persist? Some answers have already been suggested; the union's basic personality characteristics, its small size, its semi-rural location, its reason for formation, its support from employers, and so forth. This chapter explores still another explanation and possibly the major one for its persistence: the remarkable lassitude and ineptness of international union challengers.

Both the attitudes and the behavior of the internationals toward single-firm unions help explain a major feature of relations between them; namely, the limited number of such relationships. Most of the unions studied have little or nothing to do with local unions or agents of the international unions. This is particularly true of weak unions protected from such contacts by their small size, semi-rural location, and record of employee satisfaction with employer paternalism. Strong unions, on the other hand, are occasionally targets of international union raiders intrigued by the possibility of assimilating an experienced independent union with a strong treasury and a competitive labor contract. Strong independents also frequently seek ties with various local unions in an attempt to strengthen themselves and sometimes to head off a raid. Nevertheless, the absence of contacts or ties with local unions is more common than had been expected.

Lack of Contact Between International Unions and Independents. The search for an explanation of the small number of contacts between single-firm unions and their international rivals soon focused on two explanations, one somewhat superficial and easy to come by and the other more meaningful and less obvious. It was apparent from the start that the two rivals compete in very few areas. The small number of single-firm unions in the country, possibly 1,400, helps explain a lack of contact with the 78,000 locals of the nation's 180-odd international unions. Moreover, the absence of single-firm unions from the basic industries such as steel, autos, rubber, and construction where local unions are plentiful and their presence in industries such as chemicals, petroleum, and telephones where the locals are weak underline the separation of the two types of union. As they frequently represent a protest against unionism, single-firm unions can flourish only in situations with built-in checks against employer exploitation such as industries based on continuous-flow operations or those which require a highly specialized labor force.

A more meaningful and less obvious explanation focuses on a striking discrepancy between the anticipated and the actual conduct of the international unions. Contrary to expectations, the international unions do not carefully and painstakingly pursue active campaigns aimed at winning over independent unions.[1] Indeed, research established that the international union campaign against the single-firm unions have always involved more talk than action. In the late 1920's, for example, although the AFL was vociferous in its condemnation of the company union, a critic found the leaders of international unions ill-informed and inactive:

> "The writer has had occasion to write to the heads of various unions in industries where the company unions have made significant advances. Some of their replies have been a pathetic revelation of ignorance and indifference to the whole problem . . . [they reveal] considerable ignorance as to the number, types, and character of the company unions that have been introduced." [1927][2]

Similarly, when this writer surveyed fifteen large international unions in 1960 he found striking lack of knowledge and interest in the single-firm independent union.

The fifteen unions surveyed were specifically selected because single-firm unions were numerous in their jurisdiction.[3] They represented 7,500,000 members, or slightly more than half of the total number of union members in the country. Their members were organized in 14,000 locals in the fifty states. Only three of these fifteen international unions kept any record of the addresses of single-firm unions in their jurisdiction; the others were either not interested, did not feel their resources permitted such an undertaking, or delegated the function with no follow-up to their locals. Furthermore, each of the lists supplied by the three international unions contained considerably fewer unions than the writer's research uncovered in the industry involved.

When asked for details on single-firm unions, the international unions supplied only vague statements or the admission that no record was kept.[4] This was also true of state AFL-CIO organizations.[5] Typical responses from representatives of the fifteen international unions included the following:

> "Anything I would be able to gather would be from government source material which I am sure you have access to. . . ."

> "We do not have details of our organization's contact with officers of independent unions. I am certain that such details are not available anywhere. We do not keep records of our union's representation contests against independent unions. In fact, there is nowhere available within the union any single source of the record of representation elections from which information could be gathered. . . ."

> "Our contacts with single-firm independent unions are sporadic and scattered. Information about such unions, our contact with them, etc. *may* filter back to the national office, but if such information is referred back, I have not seen it. . . ."

The three international unions represented directly above had a total of 2,200,000 members in 4,600 locals in the fifty states.

This haphazard and casual approach to local union relations with single-firm unions reflects a widespread and time-honored attitude toward independent rivals.[6] The attitude was succinctly expressed 32 years ago by AFL leaders:

Relations with the Internationals

"The workers who play with the company union will very soon burn their fingers and become disillusioned. They will see that the plan is merely to betray them, that they can secure nothing substantial from it, that it is infinitely inferior to the trade union. They will thereupon return to our fold, or if they have not been trade unionists before they will suddenly see the light and come over to the real unions. In the meanwhile there is nothing that we can do except to sit tight and observe the process. No special tactics are necessary. The company unions will pass away in due season leaving us in command of the field." [1927][7]

Whether in spite of or partially because of the complacency of the AFL craft union elite, the company unions did not soon pass away, but grew instead to boast a 1935 membership half as large as the AFL's.

More recently, in 1958, wishful optimism again characterized a representative labor analysis of the independent union's future. The *Digest* of the AFL-CIO's Industrial Union Department solemnly observed that:

"As paternalism breaks down, as company human relations programs fail, and as independent unions come to voice the opinions of management, wage earners will always recognize the need for effective rather than shirt-front organizations . . . sooner or later, recognition that there is no substitute for strong, effective unionism does come."[8]

Representatives of the fifteen international unions surveyed on the subject offered views consistent with the above. For example:

"It would be an overstatement to suggest that we have any sort of plans regarding our relations with independent unions. It seems almost certain that whatever insignificant role independent unions now play, that role will continue to decrease."

"I doubt if there are any independents that are not in

some way company dominated. . . . In the last twenty-five years the number of independents has probably remained quite stable and growth has been negligible. Now with their officers getting along in years (generally the original officers are still in 'power'), we feel that these independents will be more and more interested in affiliating with bona fide trade unions. So in the next decade we foresee that almost all the independents will be swallowed up by AFL-CIO unions."

The two international unions represented above had a total combined membership of 1,600,000 workers in 4,700 locals. In this way, then, the major unions in 1960 and for thirty years previous explained their lassitude in challenging single-firm independent unions. Wishful thinking substituted for forthright action.

While casualness is the dominant characteristic of international union concern with independents, there are pressures operating in the opposite direction. The decline in union membership, both absolute and also relative to the size of the work force, puts pressure on the major unions to pay new attention to independent unions. Labor representation on such bodies as legislative advisory committees, Blue Cross Plans, university study groups, and United Fund organizations brings local union and independent union leaders into close contact. The leaders of the rival unions have had increasing occasion to join forces for a common legislative goal (such as more liberal compensation benefits). Finally, many international unions have been stirred from their lethargy in this area by the example of stunning raid victories secured by the few major unions vigorously wooing members of independents. For example, the culmination in 1961 of a long campaign by the Communications Workers of America (AFL-CIO) resulted in victory over two independent unions of 24,000 Bell Telephone workers. This was the CWA's largest such gain since the 1940's and the largest gain of any AFL-CIO international union since the merger of the AFL and CIO in 1955.[9]

There are apparently two major contact patterns: active competition and strategic cooperation. The first presents the

best publicized and most misrepresented form of contact between the two kinds of unions.* The second is the most portentous and least well-known.

Active Competition. At the heart of relations between international unions and independents is a common recognition of
rivalry. Each challenges a basic characteristic of the other, its
scope; each thinks the other unnecessary; and each feels an
obligation to "convert" the other. The single-firm unions suspect that most international unions are actively conspiring to
undermine and replace the independent labor organizations.
They wish the international unions would abandon the effort
and renounce "monopoly power," socialistic ways, racketeering,
power politics, and other ills condemned by the independents'
basic ideology and attributed by them to most international
unions. In their turn, the major unions condemn most independents as company unions and hope to convert them into
legitimate labor organizations. A spokesman for the major
unions declared in 1958:

> "Stripped of power at the bargaining table, helpless to
> conduct effective economic action, deprived of experienced
> leadership, and isolated from legislative interest, today's
> independent provides little, if any, advantage over the out-
> right company union."[10]

Attempts at winning over a single-firm union frequently take
the form of an organizational raid.[11] Typically, an international
union representative seeks to build a core of influential followers within an independent and hopes that these individuals can
command a majority vote for affiliation in a forthcoming NLRB
representation contest. A student of competition among local
unions and independents in the chemical industry notes:

> "If appeals to [local autonomy within the framework of
> an international union] fail to sway prospective members,
> the competing unions sometimes cater to the more ma-

---

* The mass media cannot be trusted as a guide to inter-union relations.
Sporadic coverage of large-scale raids gives the false impression that raids
are commonplace, usually successful, and are the only possible relationship between rival unions.

terial motivations of personal gain. In most cases there are a few key individuals in each unit who command the respect and confidence of the members . . . the leaders of independents have been put on an international's payroll as 'temporary organizers' and given further consideration for permanent positions. Indeed, the officers of independent unions have been known to demand a full-time job with the international as a condition of affiliation."[12]

The frequency of this approach is given by the fact that nearly half of the independent leaders interviewed who had beaten off a raid attempt had rejected some sort of job or assistance offer from the raider.

The newest wrinkle in the affiliation drives involves a "soft-sell" approach. In place of bitter denunciations, charges of company-domination, inflammatory leaflets, and covert offers to "influentials," many international union raiders simply request an opportunity to address a meeting of the independent union and debate calmly the merits and costs of affiliation. The request is not always granted; the leader of a weak single-firm union of 58 petroleum warehouse employees recalled that:

> "The CIO came to us in 1959 and wanted to talk at a meeting. I was not there the night the vote was taken but I understand twenty guys came and fifteen voted 'no.' They haven't bothered us since . . . they can't help us. We favor the Teamsters and we may affiliate if the three-year deadlock in negotiations doesn't break in our favor pretty soon."

Even when the request to address a meeting is granted, success for the raider is still problematic. The president of a weak union of 160 metal products employees offered this example:

> "The IUE tried to raid us two months ago. They gave out leaflets boosting themselves, but saying little about us. After a while they managed to get thirty cards signed. We gave them permission to speak at one of our meetings. They wanted us to disappear into one of their large locals. We wanted our own charter and control of our money. So they got nowhere and we haven't had any contact since."

Relations with the Internationals

Such setbacks to the side, the low cost in time, paper, and emotional energy entailed in the "soft-sell" raid make it likely that this approach will become increasingly popular.[13]

Whatever the approach, the number of raids is not great and the record of the international unions is not especially impressive. Only twenty of the forty unions studied had ever been raided, and almost all had been raided only once. While the twenty unions had been challenged in the last ten years, the majority had not been challenged in the last three years. As suggested elsewhere, these twenty unaffiliated unions were stronger, larger, wealthier, and older than most.[14] They were also exposed in urban industrial centers to international unions and were often strategically located in a key plant of a large concern.

Available NLRB figures for contests throughout the land confirmed an impression of minimal raid activity, and considerable independent union success.[15] NLRB data for 1948 through 1958 indicate an average of 140 contests annually between independents and international unions, ranging from 42 in 1958 to a peak of 198 in 1951 and down to 130 in 1958. With a population of possibly 1,400 independent single-firm unions, this suggests that less than ten per cent have been confronted by a raid every year of the past several. Moreover, the minority involved have fared quite well. They won a majority (or 54 per cent) of the elections in all years except 1953. To put it briefly, the international union is an unimpressive raider.[16]

Why is this so and what are the consequences? A representative case study offers some answers to the first of these questions.[17] In 1958 the Teamsters and several other international unions wooed a very disgruntled independent union of 1,700 oil refinery workers in Baton Rouge, Louisiana. The Teamsters brought in their President, James R. Hoffa, and spent over $200,000 in the campaign. The Oil, Chemical and Atomic Workers International Union (OCAW) brought in its President, O. A. Knight, who emphasized that his union was not only democratic and clean but was also the proper union of oil workers. The leaders of the independent union swung their support to the Teamsters and urged affiliation on the refinery workers. In December, 1959, the NLRB conducted a representation election. Ninety-five per cent of the 3,500 eligible employees voted; seventy-five per cent chose the old independent union.

To judge from this case, an international union raid might fail because of the disapproval by the community of the raider, distrust of the "turncoat" supporters of affiliation, the conduct of particular raiders, the costly demands of a serious effort, the raider's reputation as strike-prone or corrupt, the complexity of a challenger's scheme to reshape the unit, the independent unions greater familiarity with the situation, and the support of the employer for the unaffiliated union.[18] This list is only suggestive and by no means exhaustive. It makes clear a conclusion suggested by the bare NLRB statistics: the international unions are mistaken in their low estimate of the fighting and staying power of the single-firm independent unions.

Strategic Cooperation. In keeping with the drift in raids from a "hard" to a "soft-sell" approach, many international unions are reported to be interested in cooperation rather than in bitter competition with single-firm independent unions. The form of cooperation can range from annual phone calls between rival union leaders to a pre-affiliation trial of international union resources.

The notion of wooing rather than fighting independent unions was advanced as long as 38 years ago, though honored until recently more in the breach than in the observance. In 1923, Carroll E. French advised international unions to consider the early independent unions worthy of respect and cooperation. To maintain the relation of adversaries would only handicap the effort to unite the "labor movement."[19] Similarly, 15 years ago another scholar wrote:

> "Fighting these insurgents [the independent union] and trying to discredit them will never dissolve their doubts. Sympathy and help may win them over. . . . Antagonism and misrepresentation will never accomplish that objective. The example of sound trade unionism, an educational campaign and actual assistance, for instance at the time of a strike, would be the real persuader."[20]

More recently, in 1958, a publication of the AFL-CIO noted:

Relations with the Internationals

"Under today's circumstances, it has become increasingly difficult to contest established independents. Many unions, however, have been able to work with well-intentioned independent union leaders and this has proven to be one way toward merging them into the legitimate trade union movement."[21]

In short, as a result either of a poor record in competitive raids, or new sophistication in inter-union relations, or just plain weariness among aging international union representatives, the olive-branch and brief-case have replaced the purple leaflet and brickbat in many international union contacts with independents.

This cooperative relation involves the deliberate establishment of friendly, first-name contact between independent and local union leaders, the exchange of information, joint attendance at ceremonial or social affairs, and rare pledges of moral or financial aid in times of crisis. For example, a student of union relations in the chemical industry has noted that:

"To induce affiliation, the international may provide the independent with a sample of its services before the latter has taken formal steps to change its status. Such offers of aid are frequently made when the independent is in a crisis situation in collective bargaining and the inadequacies of its own resources are most apparent. In one instance, an [international union] official went so far as to help an independent union to negotiate a new contract. This independent was so pleased with the service that the international official was recommended to another unaffiliated local in another plant of the same company."[22]

This sort of cooperative relationship is often initiated by an independent union that seeks to head off active competition by offering to participate in an alternative arrangement. Wise local union officials recognize the valuable entre offered into independent affairs, and generally welcome the arrangement. The real winners are rank-and-filers afforded a chance for careful comparison by a guarded but peaceful inter-union alliance.

On rare occasions an independent will initiate such a relationship not as a defensive move but for the purpose of advanc-

117

Relations with the Internationals

ing its fortunes as an independent union. For example, the leader of a strong union of 1,400 rubber workers revealed that:

". . . for the past five years I have been going with representatives of the Textile Workers international union on annual visits to one of the company's four unorganized plants. The company doesn't know anything about this. I do it because only five of the company's nine plants are organized. Until we have unions in all nine plants nobody but the company benefits. There is no sentiment for independents in the unorganized plants, so I push the next best thing, a good international."

Similarly, the president of a weak union of 320 chemical company employees explained:

"We used to be in a company-wide federation of independent unions back from 1954 through 1956. . . . We think we have a better deal now with our area dinners. When it comes time for us to bargain a new contract we foot the bill for a dinner that brings together representatives from five independents and three AFL-CIO locals in nearby chemical companies."

Such initiative on the part of independents is not rare, particularly when a leader is a dynamic individual or a union is seeking to strengthen its weak position.

Two final comments are in order. The number of cooperative relationships is fairly small and few unions regard the relationship as anything more than a polite variation on active competition. That is, the parties seldom forget that theirs is basically a relationship of rivals. Both parties share responsibility for the limited number of alliances. Many international unions refuse to discriminate among independent unions and prefer to condemn all as "company unions" not worthy of attention. Many believe a cooperative relationship only delays the imminent collapse of the independent union and refuse therefore to help their supposedly ailing rival. On their part, some independents simply prefer conflict to cooperation; both their personnel and their organizational philosophy are geared

118

to suspicion and contests, and not to trust and cooperative efforts. Others think the risks entailed not worth the possible advantages. Many independent union leaders fear such relations would not only show up shortcomings in their unions but possibly even their personal shortcomings as leaders. Whatever the explanation, in all of these cases the real losers are the rank-and-filers, both local union and independent union members.

Consequences. Lack of contact with the international unions aid some independents by providing "an insulation of ignorance." Members are not troubled by first-hand knowledge of local union resources, gains, and goals. They are protected from discontent with their own union by ignorance of comparative standards. Leaders have the opportunity to malign the absent challenger and to champion pet programs as vital for defense in "impending" raids. On the other hand, lack of contact with local unions can weaken independent unions by depressing goals, encouraging a debilitating feeling of isolation, and supporting extreme naivete concerning comparative union performance. This naivete can leave a union especially vulnerable to its first contact with an international union raider and the raider's often extravagant claims. On balance, however, the independent union most frequently isolated from local unions, the weak single-firm union, seems more secure in its isolation than otherwise.

The second most common relationship of independent unions and international unions involves active competition. Raids are generally unsuccessful, but there are some common consequences of raids for the victorious independent. The union may initiate reforms directed at correcting faults exposed and exploited by the raider.[23] An example is available in the Baton Rouge union discussed in the preceding case study. This union followed its victory by raising dues from one dollar to two dollars per member per month. The move was taken to strengthen the union treasury, enhance its ability to strike, and enable it to hire full-time officers and part-time staff assistance. Certain unions find the fact of a raid helpful in securing extra concessions from an employer anxious to preserve them as independents. Raids generally create an atmosphere of tension which union leaders can use to secure their positions, silence opposition, and unite the membership.[24] Victory can be used to instill in dues-payers a vital sense of confidence. The president of a weak union of 98 rubber company employees reported:

"Raids don't frighten us. We started our union in 1955 because we did not want to join the CIO Rubber Workers and we beat them 87 to 13 in the election. When they came back and raided us in 1957 we beat them 85 to 12. If they come again, we will beat them again. We're a small company with everyone members of one big family. They don't offer us anything, and we all know this."

Many other independent union leaders similarly feel invigorated by past challenges and equal to future ones.

On the other hand, a raid may have negative after-effects even though the independent wins the ballot count. Exposed faults may defy correction short of affiliation. For example, correcting the "fault" of inadequate staff services demands a dues increase that brings largest returns only if channeled to a staff-conscious international union. Personal feuds between pro- and anti-affiliation forces may linger. In this connection, the leader of a strong union of 1,500 chemical company employees explained:

"The man I beat this year for the presidency had held the post for eight years. It was a close and bitter election; I only won by 35 votes with 1,100 ballots cast. . . . He was pro-CIO and lost votes because we rejected the CIO by two-to-one in a raid six months ago . . . the darts really flew during the campaign. My supporters got so enraged over his tactics (the incumbent) that we labeled him a 'bleeding cancer.' He gave us as good as he got. . . . I'm left with a split administration. I've got to work somehow with the old president's secretary and treasurer. He has retained support among the delegates . . . my supporters see plots everywhere and we are suspicious of everyone. There is no saying how this is going to end."

The employer's behavior, whether in support of the independent union or otherwise, may alienate some unionists.[25] A some-

Relations with the Internationals

what extreme but illuminating case was offered by the head of a weak union of 21 machine shop employees:

> "The UAW has been trying to win us over since we formed our own union two years ago. At that time the UAW tried to force an election. The company got frightened and told us we were better for every one concerned than an outside union. A vice-president of the company let it be known that he could buy off a local president of the UAW, and this hurt the supporters of affiliation. The company also said it would cut its support of our medical insurance if the UAW won. This was nothing compared with the fact that the company used one of the workers to spy on the guys that favored the outside union. The guys were wise to the spy and fed him false information. There is still some bad feeling over this, and we may go UAW in another few months."

The requirements of raid defenses may hamper the operation of other union programs that hold membership support. The same dollars cannot be used both to print leaflets against affiliation and to subsidize a traditional Christmas party in the shop. Finally, the independent union's defensive tactics may impress shop members as offensive. For example, many independent union constitutions contain very rigorous clauses designed to impede the affiliation process.[26] A raid calls attention to these generally ignored proscriptions and may stir resentment over legalistic hindrances to the swift and easy expression of "majority will."

It is exceedingly difficult to know beforehand whether the consequences of a victory will prove an aid to the union's viability. A raid does not end with a ballot count, the basic rivalry between the independent and the local union runs too deep for that. On balance, however, active competition is not immediately or exceptionally harmful to the nation's single-firm independent unions. Indeed, the *myth* of an international union threat as well as the harmless facts of such contacts helps the independent unions persevere.

Like the others, the last and rarest of the relationships between the independent unions and the local unions, the pattern

121

Relations with the Internationals

of strategic cooperation, offers aid or hindrance. Unions can win valuable bargaining gains through new-found strength, cast off flattering illusions about international unions, and undertake a rigorous "home-trial" of affiliation advantages without abandoning unaffiliated status. On the other hand, cooperating independents can be overly impressed by special efforts the major unions pass off as "standard." Cooperating unions also risk splitting their membership between those who want to pursue the relationship further and those who feel a definite danger of affiliation in such a course. In practice, however, as in the case of no contact or a contest, most cooperative relationships have positive effects in strengthening the independents. This is due largely to the lassitude and ineptness of international union challengers.

International unions apparently overestimate the weakness of the single-firm unions. Most internationals await the collapse of the independents. The infrequent raids on the independent unions are apt to be unsuccessful. Despite a change from harsh to polite raids, the record clearly establishes the ineptness of the raiders and the staying power of the independents. Despite a change in some cases from indifference or hostility to cooperation the record suggests that independent unions remain wary, wily, and worthy parties to a relationship that has not threatened their persistence.

FOOTNOTES

1. The expectation of contact between the rivals was encouraged, for example, by comments in Taft, Philip, "Independent Unions and the Merger," *Industrial and Labor Relations Review*, 9 (April, 1956), p. 445; and Troy, Leo, "Local Independent Unions and the American Labor Movement," *Industrial and Labor Relations Review*, 14 (April, 1961), p. 346.

2. Dunn, Robert W., *Company Unions: Employers' 'Industrial Democracy'* (New York: Vanguard Press, 1927), p. 185. Dunn criticized the lax AFL campaign and blamed AFL reluctance to sponsor industrial unions for the success of the company unions. *Ibid.*, pp. 184-206. See

Relations with the Internationals

also Wander, Paul, "The Challenge of Company-Made Unionism," *American Labor Dynamics*, J. B. S. Hardman, ed. (New York: Harcourt, Brace and Co., 1928), pp. 226-244. At the time, however, some AFL leaders believed that "after disillusionment a bona fide labor union would take over the company unions en masse; that the bosses were only doing an organizing job for the unions." Shefferman, Nathan W. (with Dale Kramer), *The Man in the Middle* (New York: Doubleday and Co., Inc., 1961), p. 84.

3. The international unions included: the Amalgamated Clothing Workers, the International Association of Machinists, the International Brotherhood of Electrical Workers, the International Brotherhood of Pulp, Sulphite, and Paper Mill Workers; the International Brotherhood of Teamsters; the International Chemical Workers, the International Ladies' Garment Workers' Union, the International Union of Electrical, Radio, and Machine Workers; the Communication Workers; the Oil, Chemical, and Atomic Workers; the Retail Clerks International Association, the Textile Workers Union, the United Automobile Workers, the United Rubber Workers, and the United Steelworkers. The statistics on size of union and number of locals are from U.S. Department of Labor, *Directory of National and International Labor Unions in the United States, 1959* (Washington, D.C.: Bureau of Labor Statistics, Bulletin No. 1267, December, 1959).

4. Among other things the international unions were asked for the mailing addresses of independent unions in the jurisdiction, details of contacts with these unions, the win-loss record in raids on these unions, and international union's concept of the independent union's future and the international's role in that future.

5. The writer interviewed officers of both state AFL and state CIO bodies in New Jersey and Pennsylvania (four groups in all). He has no reason to suspect that replies were unrepresentative of those he might have received from other state bodies (such as AFL-CIO state bodies that were merged at the time).

6. Note that a new index to international union periodicals has listed only 20 or so references to independents from its first issue, January, 1960, through the latest available edition, January, 1962. The index regularly covers 40 or more international union publications; the listings for any single month include several hundred articles. Bureau of Industrial Relations, *The University of Michigan Index of Labor Union Periodicals* (Ann Arbor, Michigan: Bureau of Industrial Relations, University of Michigan).

7. Dunn, *op. cit.*, p. 185.

8. "Independent of Whom?" *IUD Digest*, Summer 1958, p. 79. Note that major union dependence on the independent's eventual "withering away" ignores the fact that weak independents are coerced or bribed away from affiliation, that strong independents are only mildly interested, and that insecure independents might welcome reasonable overtures *if* they were reached in a certain way at the right time. A single approach, in short, is wrong—wrong that is, for the international unions.

9. "CWA Chalks Up Two Big Election Victories in N.Y.," *CWA News*, April, 1961, p. 1. See also "USW Cracks Ohio Plant," *Business Week*, February 3, 1962, p. 46; "Armco Steel Workers Vote to Keep Their Independent Union," *Business Week*, March 31, 1962, p. 82.

Relations with the Internationals

10. *IUD Digest, op. cit.*

11. For examples of the old bitter raid, see Sayles, Leonard R. and Strauss, George, *The Local Union* (New York: Harper & Brothers, 1953), pp. 151-152; Strauss, George, "Factors in the Unionization of a Utilities Company: A Case Study," *Human Organization*, 12 (Fall 1953), pp. 17-25; Purcell, Theodore V., S.J., *The Worker Speaks His Mind* (Cambridge, Mass.: Harvard University Press, 1953); Purcell, Theodore V., *Blue Collar Man* (Cambridge, Mass.: Harvard University Press, 1960), pp. 21, 24, *passim*.

12. Weber, Arnold R., "Competitive Unionism in the Chemical Industry," *Industrial and Labor Relations Review*, 13 (October, 1959), p. 29. "The appeal to personal gain, as a dimension of competition, stems from a pragmatic appreciation of the difficulties of growth and survival in an environment where politics may be more important than principle." *Ibid.*

13. See "NLRB Run-Off in Downstate, N.Y. between CWA and Independent," *CWA News*, March, 1961, p. 2; "IUE Opens White Collar Drives at National Cash Register, Frigidaire," *Engineering Employment Practices Newsletter*, April, 1961, p. 3. New attention to white-collar organization probably explains much of the "soft-sell" development. The "soft-sell," however, is also used in blue-collar campaigns. See "USW Cracks Antiunion Area," *IUD Bulletin*, February, 1962, p. 15. Integral to the new raid style is the willingness of the raider to adapt its structure to the needs of independent. See for example *Boilermakers Blacksmiths Journal*, February, 1960, p. 25.

14. Krislov offers indirect evidence for the notion that strong, large independents are more often raid targets than weak, small organizations. Krislov, Joseph, "The Extent and Trends of Raiding Among American Unions," *Quarterly Journal of Economics*, 69 (February, 1955), p. 151.

15. NLRB data is taken from Troy, *op. cit.* The writer also interviewed key NLRB officials in Washington, D.C. For a detailed analysis of NLRB data, see Troy, Leo, "The Course of Company and Local Independent Unions" (Unpublished Doctoral Dissertation, Columbia University, 1958). Note that figures from the only state (New York) that provides data on state contests complement conclusions suggested by NLRB data. See New York State Labor Relations Board, *Twenty-First Annual Analysis of Decisions* (New York, N.Y.: N.Y. S.L.R.B., 1958), p. 88.

16. Troy finds that for 1948-1959 inclusive, independents repelled local-initiated raids an average of 54 per cent of the time and defeated locals in raids initiated by the independents an average of 63 per cent of the time. Troy, *Industrial and Labor Relations Review, op. cit.* Krislov finds that for 1940-1952, "except for 1946, the local independents have been successful in about two-thirds of their raids against affiliated unions." Krislov, Joseph, "Raiding Among the 'Legitimate' Unions," *Industrial and Labor Relations Review*, 8 (October, 1954), p. 20. In a later article, Krislov noted a rise in the number of elections initiated by independents from 18 per cent of all contests in 1940 and 1943 to about 55 per cent in 1955 and 1958. "Similarly, in 1940 and 1943 the local independents won 31 contests—approximately 30 per cent; in 1955 and 1958 the local independents won 25 contests—approximately 57 per cent." Krislov, Joseph, "Organizational Rivalry Among American Unions," *Industrial and Labor Relations Review*, 13 (January, 1960), p. 219.

Relations with the Internationals

17. See Marshall, F. Ray, "Independent Unions in the Gulf Coast Petroleum Refining Industry—The Esso Experience," *Labor Law Journal,* September 1961, pp. 823-840. See also "New Names in CPI's Labor Line-Up," *Chemical Week,* February 3, 1962, pp. 45-46.

18. The list might also include the independent's suspicion that its interests will suffer at the hands of wily leaders of the international unions. Similarly, the president of an independent of 35 oil truck drivers told the writer that the union would never affiliate so long as major unions insisted on equal job rights for Negroes, a policy contrary to the employer's.

19. French, Carroll E., *The Shop Committee in the United States* (Baltimore, Maryland: The Johns Hopkins Press, 1923), p. 104. Morris has uncovered evidence that AFL leaders in the 1920's seriously considered reaching a rapprochement with rival company union leaders—though out of AFL weakness, rather than strength. Morris, James O., *Conflict Within the AFL* (Ithaca, N.Y.: Cornell University, 1958), p. 70.

20. Smith, William J., S.J., *Spotlight on Labor Unions* (New York: Duell, Sloan and Pearce, 1946), p. 48.

21. *IUD Digest, op. cit.* See also Curran, Joseph, "The President's Column," *The Pilot,* April 2, 1953, p. 9; "Esso Conference in Washington," *The International Teamster,* April, 1959, pp. 7-8; "Teamsters Lend Aid to Refinery Workers," *Ibid.,* pp. 5-6, 9; "Vermont Independent Union Wins 9¢ Strike Settlement," *UE News,* July 3, 1961, p. 3.

22. Weber, *op. cit.,* p. 26.

23. Brooks applauds the frequent contribution of union rivalry to improved union service and the opportunity it offers dues-payers to withdraw support from an unsatisfactory representative. Brooks, George W., *The Sources of Vitality in the American Labor Movement* (Ithaca, N.Y.: N. Y. School of Industrial and Labor Relations, Bulletin No. 41, 1960), pp. 29-33. Weber, on the other hand, finds competitive unionism in the chemical industry has resulted in wasteful, inefficient utilization of resources, has afforded management important tactical advantages in collective bargaining, and has not provided the stimulus for significant innovations in trade union policy and practice. Weber, *op. cit.,* pp. 35, 37. Barbash concludes that "rival unionism has no inherent relationship to democracy in the rival unions or to the quality of the union performance." Barbash, Jack, *Labor's Grass Roots* (New York: Harper & Brothers, 1961), p. 229.

24. A raid puts an unusual strain on harassed leaders: it may not be a coincidence that the first suit ever brought by the Secretary of Labor against a union for election malpractices involved an independent wracked by factionalism brought on by a raid. See "Oil Industry 'Independent' Faces Court in Election Case," *AFL-CIO News,* September 17, 1960, p. 4.

25. Employer support for a raid-harassed independent is common—if usually subtly employed. *Business Week* notes ". . . nobody doubts that they prefer independents in their plants, not the [Steelworkers Union]." However, as Taft-Hartley places them "on the sidelines," the employers "can't play favorites." "USW Grabs at Independents," *Business Week,* April 8, 1961, p. 60. Similarly, while Marshall notes some employer displeasure with the naïvete of independents, he concludes that "the employers are not willing to sacrifice the power advantages of dealing with independents," Marshall, *op. cit.,* p. 840.

Relations with the Internationals

26. Examination of over 400 constitutions revealed frequent use of an extended schedule of meetings, a high minimum vote for consideration and even higher votes for action, and the residing of veto power in a small minority in the matter of affiliation. Weber cites a single case of "difficult" affiliation provisions as evidence that "these unions are not always exemplars of internal democracy." Weber, *op. cit.*, p. 33.

X. THE FUTURE OF THE
SINGLE-FIRM INDEPENDENT UNION

THERE is no question of the single-firm union replacing the country's international labor organizations. As made clear in previous chapters the independents have no appeal in industries characterized by horizontal job mobility or joint employer action, and the independents cannot match such features of the major unions as vast research facilities, large treasuries, considerable political influence, and the like. The limitations of the situation of the independents in combination with the special virtues of these organizations gives rise to a number of revealing paradoxes. These in turn contain vital clues to the future of America's forgotten labor organizations, a future that can involve a healthy supplemental relationship of international and independent unions.

Paradoxes. The weak independent unions are the most secure unions. These small organizations, located far from the big city centers of the international unions, have little to attract the predatory interest of major union raiders and have much to recommend their support by management. Everything about them is on a small scale: their resources, their membership, their influence and their goals. The workers they represent do not identify their interests with those of labor in general. They feel no pressing need for the many services the weak unions do not provide and would object to any increase in their low dues or in the few demands made on them.

The strong independent unions are the most threatened unions. Their very strength puts them in danger from two opposing directions: from the major international unions who are attracted by a large membership and a wealthy treasury and from managers who are not sympathetic to a demanding, self-reliant union. Moreover, the interest these unions display in providing a wide range of services, in engaging in political action and community affairs, and in influencing public opinion, coincide more closely with the interests of the major unions than with those of the typical weak independent union. Even if the raids of major unions on the strong independents

127

are not immediately successful, affiliation remains a probable future for many of them.

The unions most committed to preserving independent status are the most interested in affiliation with other independents. As they are the most threatened, the strong independent unions are the most in need of aid. They have clutched at the straw of association with other independent unions only to discover it will not bear the weight of the problems they face. Since their principal advantage over the international unions is individual autonomy, each of the unions is reluctant to surrender much of that autonomy; but the associations are doomed to ineffectiveness without the whole-hearted support of their affiliates. In the end, members find themselves weakly supporting a powerless association instead of gaining powerful aid from a strongly-supported one.

Office staffs and professional engineers are increasing in the nation's labor force, but independent unions of these workers are declining in numbers. Most such unions were formed just after World War II when the union movement was at peak strength in the United States. They were not organized to combat exploitation by unscrupulous employers, nor do they now have such a strong reason for remaining organized. On the contrary, employers of white-collar employees usually display an active interest in their employees' welfare. An equally important reason for the decline in the unions of white-collar employees is the traditional hostility of such workers to any form of labor organization for themselves.

The final paradox of the single-firm independent union is that its very character is the source of its jeopardy. At a time when the dealings between labor and management are everywhere characterized by consolidation—with contracts negotiated between a single giant union and a combination of its many employers, with mergers of unions themselves into still larger organizations—the independence of the single-firm union makes it something of an anachronism. Its emphasis on leadership from its ranks handicaps it in dealing with the increasing professionalism of management in industry. Its focus on the plant and the employer to the exclusion of interest in public affairs and the labor movement in general means that it is

The Future of the Unions

overlooked by politicians and labor specialists. Its conservatism robs it of the possibility of rallying support for exciting issues.

An Appraisal. The fact that the single-firm union operates under difficulties does not mean that it is without virtue. It epitomizes an ideal of Jeffersonian democracy: that individuals must take responsibility for matters important to them. It gives the union rank-and-file a rare opportunity to speak and be heard. In this era of decision by committees and experts, it allows "little men" a rare opportunity to help shape their own work lives. Its independence makes it free of outside pressures and permits it to display ingenuity and flexibility in dealing with new problems of technology and plant-dispersion. When it negotiates with strength and vigor, it provides a genuine alternative to membership in certain international unions. Everyone involved gains from this kind of competition. (Even the weak independent union that chooses to make itself a servile tool of the employers' decisions brings some experience of unionism to members who would otherwise remain in the ignorance of isolation.) It rejects the traditional hostility between management and labor in favor of cooperation to achieve the goals held in common, an attitude reflecting its special industrial setting. Only the most successful and far-sighted international unions have managed to gain such maturity of viewpoint in industrial relations.

The immediate future of the single-firm independent union is not auspicious. There is likely to be a decline in the total number of such unions and in the membership they represent. Every new management association and every new contract negotiated for a whole industry encourages employees to join large-scale major unions rather than small independent ones. Similarly, the standardization of management policies favors the internationals. A new class of work-force entrants will be better-educated and more highly-skilled than workers in the past and will be committed to a higher standard of living. They will demand of their unions the services available only from powerful international union organizations. The internationals themselves have begun to custom-design their approach to the independent union members, and their new concerted

The Future of the Unions

"soft-sell" technique may make greater inroads on the present membership of independents than the infrequent bitter raids of the past.

The proportion of weak independent unions to strong is likely to increase in the future. The new independents will probably appear in small out-of-the-way shops, as the major unions focus on large urban locations. Such independent unions are almost always weak bargainers. As there is little likelihood of a stepped-up legal campaign against domination, the safety of the new weak unions is assured. The very strength of the strong unions makes them more threatened by major unions while the small weak independents are protected by their limited goals, their lack of appeal to international union raiders and their small-scale employers.

There is still time to preserve the nation's single-firm independent unions and to increase their effectiveness. Rather than being left to exist as pale modern versions of company unions, the independents can be charged with the responsibility of keeping the standards of unionism high. They can be charged with the responsibility of deserving a mutually beneficial relationship with the major unions. Weak independents can resolve to free themselves of a degrading servile dependency and strong independents can resolve to eschew unrealistic goals and to strengthen their multi-union associations. These courses of action demand much from all involved: members will have to approve strengthening the program and finances of their organizations, and will have to volunteer more time and effort. Employers and the general public will be pressed to accommodate the more virile behavior and more trying demands of the revived independents. In balance, however, as the labor policy of the nation makes clear, the parties will all profit from a reinvigorated relationship of autonomous and responsible bargainers.

The situation at present leaves much to be desired; weak independents are pitiful and strong independents are hard-pressed. The immediate future is not auspicious. What is laudable in the independents is in jeopardy, while much that has been censurable from their development sixty years ago threatens to distinguish the independent unions of still another era.

The Future of the Unions

There is still time for the unions themselves to check the flow of events and to resolve that the strong, and not the weak union will characterize tomorrow's single-firm organization. Only the unions can finally determine whether they will remain America's forgotten labor organizations, or will instead realize the promise that has always been inherent in their best aspects.

The Future of the Unions

TABLE 1

Distribution of Single-Firm Independent Unions
by State: 1952[1]

Northeastern		Rocky Mountain	
New York	314	Texas	66
Pennsylvania	229	Missouri	39
Ohio	206	Louisiana	32
New Jersey	188	Oklahoma	19
Massachusetts	102	Iowa	16
Connecticut	33	Kansas	14
Maryland	30	Arkansas	4
Rhode Island	23	Colorado	3
Virginia	20	Nebraska	1
West Virginia	16	New Mexico	1
Kentucky	14		
Maine	13		
New Hampshire	7		
Delaware	7	Western	
Vermont	2	California	100
		Washington	13
Great Lakes		Oregon	10
Illinois	117	Utah	10
Indiana	60	Montana	6
Wisconsin	60	Hawaii	4
Michigan	56	Idaho	1
Minnesota	24	Alaska	1
		Arizona	1
Southeastern			
Tennessee	19		
Georgia	10	Others	
Florida	10	Puerto Rico	1
Alabama	6		
North Carolina	5		
Mississippi	3		
South Carolina	3	Total	1,919

[1] U.S. Wage Stabilization Board. *Directory of Independent Unions.*
Washington, D.C.: Wage Stabilization Board, Office of Independent
Unions, 1952. Note that multi-firm unions are included in this count, but
in unknown numbers.

The Future of the Unions

Distribution of Single-Firm Independent Unions
by State: 1960[1]

Northeastern		Rocky Mountain	
Pennsylvania	171	Missouri	48
New York	148	Texas	46
Ohio	126	Louisiana	26
New Jersey	95	Iowa	10
Massachusetts	61	Kansas	10
Maryland	19	Colorado	6
Connecticut	16	Oklahoma	6
West Virginia	16	Nebraska	2
Kentucky	14	New Mexico	2
Virginia	14	Arkansas	1
Rhode Island	8	North Dakota	0
Maine	7	South Dakota	0
New Hampshire	3	Wyoming	0
Delaware	2		
Vermont	2	Western	
		California	79
Great Lakes		Oregon	20
		Washington	13
Illinois	70	Montana	7
Michigan	42	Utah	5
Indiana	40	Hawaii	4
Wisconsin	36	Idaho	3
Minnesota	16	Alaska	3
		Nevada	2
		Arizona	1
Southeastern			
Tennessee	9	Others	
Florida	8		
Alabama	6	Puerto Rico	34
North Carolina	4	District of Columbia	3
South Carolina	4	Virgin Islands	1
Georgia	3		
Mississippi	0	Total	1,272

[1] Bureau of Labor-Management Reports. *Register of Reporting Labor Organizations* (Washington, D.C.: U.S. Department of Labor, 1960). Note that multi-firm unions are included in this count, but in unknown numbers.

SELECTED BIBLIOGRAPHY

While studies of the single-firm independent union are comparatively few in number and many are dated and unavailable, there are notable exceptions. The most valuable of these are listed here and a brief explanation is given of why they warrant special mention.

A number of the good labor studies of the time include discussion of the three predecessors of contemporary single-firm unions: the shop committees of the 1900's, the employee representation plans of the 1920's, and the company unions of the 1930's. The following are especially useful:

French, Carroll E. *The Shop Committee in the United States* (Baltimore, Maryland: The Johns Hopkins Press, 1923). A rare academic discussion of the strong and weak points of the shop committee.

Dunn, Robert W. *Company Unions: Employers' 'Industrial Democracy'* (New York: Vanguard Press, 1927). A Marxist critique which censors the AFL almost as much as the employers.

Wander, Paul. "The Challenge of Company-Made Unionism." *American Labor Dynamics*, J. B. S. Hardman, ed. (New York: Harcourt, Brace and Co., 1938), pp. 226-244. A theoretical discussion of the challenge of single-firm unit-wide organization to narrow AFL craft organization.

Millis, Harry A., ed. *How Collective Bargaining Works: A Survey of Experience in Leading American Industries* (New York: The Twentieth Century Fund, 1942). The collected essays record the peak years in the 1930's and the collapse in the 1940's of most company unions.

Bernstein, Irving. *The Lean Years: A History of the American Worker: 1920-1933* (Boston, Massachusetts: Houghton Mifflin Co., 1960). An account of the environment that supported the predecessors of contemporary single-firm organizations.

In passing it is interesting to note that the farther away one gets in time from the predecessors the less kind the critical

Selected Bibliography

verdict of students. (Bernstein, among others, is harsher than French and most of his contemporaries.)

It is not possible to leave the topic of the union predecessors without mention of a distinguished government study:

U.S. Department of Labor. *Characteristics of Company Unions* (Washington, D.C.: U.S. Bureau of Labor Statistics, Bulletin 634, 1938), 313 pp. One of the most thorough such studies ever prepared in or outside of government. It is exceedingly unfortunate that with such a fine start the Government nevertheless abandoned its study of the single-firm union in 1938 and had only this year (1962) re-initiated its research.

Some recent studies of the contemporary single-firm union consider the general case for and against these organizations; others concentrate on one or another particular industrial setting or on the status of particular memberships. The general studies include:

Anon. "The Case for the Local Independent Union." *Personnel*, 32 (November, 1955), pp. 226-234. An account of the union's merits from the employer's viewpoint.

Taft, Philip. "Independent Unions and the Merger." *Industrial and Labor Relations Review*, 9 (April, 1956), pp. 433-447. The discussion features realistic estimates of total membership and rather controversial predictions of a decline in the union's fortunes.

Anon. "Independents Begin to Huddle." *Fortune* (March, 1956), pp. 203, 206. A general overview which features rare (and critical) comments on the national associations of single-firm unions.

Anon. "Independent of Whom?" *IUD Digest* (Summer 1958), pp. 74-79. An estimate of the union's shortcomings from the viewpoint of the international unions.

Troy, Leo. "Local Independent and National Unions: Competitive Labor Organizations," *The Journal of Political Economy*, LXVIII (October, 1960), pp. 487-506. An economist argues that independence primarily reflects a belief that wage rates can be maximized by localized bargaining.

Selected Bibliography

Troy, Leo. "Local Independent Unions and the American Labor Movement." *Industrial and Labor Relations Review*, 14 (April, 1961), pp. 331-350. An economist argues that legal and economic conditions insure independent unions are all strong unions.

These studies present a wide range of viewpoints, and taken together, give a good picture of the issues involved.

Studies of independent unions in particular industries include the following:

Barbash, Jack. *Unions and Telephones*. (New York: Harper & Brothers, 1952.) An account of how and why independent unions formed the National Federation of Telephone Workers and later converted this association into an international union.

Purcell, Theodore V., S. J. *The Worker Speaks His Mind on Company and Union* (Cambridge, Mass.: Harvard University Press, 1953). The study includes the history of the major independent union in the meatpacking industry. Considerable attention is paid evaluations of the union offered by old-timers in the workforce.

Weber, Arnold R., "Competitive Unionism in the Chemical Industry." *Industrial and Labor Relations Review*, 13 (October, 1959), pp. 16-37. In addition to thoroughly examining relevant independent unions, the writer points up the few rewards and many shortcomings of inter-union rivalry.

Purcell, Theodore V., S.J. *Blue Collar Man* (Cambridge, Mass.: Harvard University Press, 1960). The study includes a rare comparison of an independent union with two serious rival locals. The independent, the National Brotherhood of Packinghouse Workers, is an organization of Swift Company employees.

Marshall, F. Ray. "Independent Unions in the Gulf Coast Petroleum Refining Industry—The Esso Experience." *Labor Law Journal* (September, 1961), pp. 823-840. While basically a case study of the failure of a Teamster Union raid, the study ranges far and explores the reasons for continued dominance of the petroleum refining industry by independent unions.

Selected Bibliography

Two relevant government offerings, although dated, contain much that is not available elsewhere:

Labor-Management Relations in the Bell Telephone System. Hearings Before the Subcommittee on Labor Management Relations of the Committee on Labor and Public Welfare. U.S. Senate, 81st Congress (Washington, D.C.: U.S. Government Printing Office, 1950). The hearings include statements by all sides in an area rife with controversy. Most striking is the call for anti-trust action by the independent unions and the opposite cry for enforced centralization of labor negotiations by the industry's major international union.

Labor-Management Relations in the East Coast Oil Tanker Industry. Hearings Before the Committee on Labor and Public Welfare. U.S. Senate, 81st Congress (Washington, D.C.: U.S. Government Printing Office, 1950). The testimony, from witnesses on all sides, includes rare discussion of labor spies, unsavory legal practices, bitter company opposition to international unions, and calculated company support of independent labor organizations.

These government hearings, of course, must be read cautiously, as the testimony is often contradictory and is almost always self-serving.

Research on independent unions of white-collar workers and professionals is exceedingly rare. Prominent in this respect are the following:

Waters, Elinor. "Unionization of Office Employees." *The Journal of Business,* xxvii (October, 1954), pp. 285-292. Some attention is paid to independent unions of office workers and the writer predicts a long future for the organizations.

Shea, T. E. "The Implications of Engineering Unionism—Western Electric Experience." *Research Management,* II (Autumn, 1959), pp. 149-157. An account of the rise and fall of a militant union of engineers as seen from management's position.

Goldstein, Bernard. "The Perspective of Unionized Professionals." *Social Forces,* 37 (May, 1959), pp. 323-327. The

Selected Bibliography

writer contends that unionized engineers have a unique definition of the important features of trade unionism, one that sustains an amalgam of elements of the professional society and the traditional trade union.

Walton, Richard E. *The Impact of the Professional Engineering Union* (Boston, Mass.: Harvard Business School, 1961). A study of actual experience with collective bargaining between employers and independent and affiliated unions representing the professional engineers of 11 concerns. The writer argues that these unions are special cases that deserve special treatment and possibly even appreciation from management.

With the changing nature of the workforce and the intensification of pressure on the international unions to devise means of organizing white-collar employees it is reasonable to expect more literature in the near future on the single-firm independent organizations.

RESEARCH PROJECTS OF THE INDUSTRIAL RELATIONS SECTION

Industrialism and Industrial Man. By Clark Kerr, John T. Dunlop, Frederick Harbison and Charles A. Myers. 1960. 331 pp. $6.00. (Published by Harvard University Press.)

The Wage-Price Issue. A Theoretical Analysis. By William G. Bowen. 1960. 447 pp. $8.50. (Published by Princeton University Press.)

Management in the Industrial World. An International Analysis. By Frederick Harbison and Charles A. Myers. 1959. 413 pp. $7.00. (Published by McGraw-Hill Book Company.)

Authority and Organization in German Management. By Heinz Hartmann. 1959. 318 pp. $6.00. (Published by Princeton University Press.)

Human Resources for Egyptian Enterprise. By Frederick Harbison and Ibrahim A. Ibrahim. 1958. 230 pp. $5.50. (Published by McGraw-Hill Book Company.)

As Unions Mature. An Analysis of the Evolution of American Unionism. By Richard A. Lester. 1958. 171 pp. $3.75. (Published by Princeton University Press.)

Reports
(Published by the Industrial Relations Section)

America's Forgotten Labor Organization. A Survey of the Role of the Single-Firm Independent Union in American Industry. Research Report No. 103. 1962. 140 pp. Paperbound $3.00; clothbound $3.75.

Enterprise and Politics in South Africa. Report Series No. 102. 1962. 102 pp. $3.00.

The Economics of Unemployment Compensation. Report Series No. 101. 1962. 130 pp. Paperbound $3.00; clothbound $3.75.

Wage Behavior in the Postwar Period. An Empirical Analysis. Report Series No. 100. 1960. 139 pp. $3.00.

The Scientist in American Industry. Some organizational determinants in manpower utilization. Report Series No. 99. 1960. 160 pp. $3.00.

High-Level Manpower in Overseas Subsidiaries. Experience in Brazil and Mexico. Report Series No. 98. 1960. 161 pp. $3.00.

Unions in America. A British view. Report Series No. 97. 1959. 136 pp. $2.00.

High-Talent Manpower for Science and Industry. An appraisal of policy at home and abroad. Report Series No. 95. 1957. 98 pp. $3.00.

Bibliographies

Manpower Problems in Economic Development. Bibliographical Series No. 85. 1958. 93 pp. $2.00.

Incentive Wage Systems. Bibliographical Series No. 83. (Revised) 1956. 24 pp. 50 cents.

A Trade Union Library. Bibliographical Series No. 84. (Revised) 1955. 58 pp. $1.50.

Complete list of available publications will be sent on request.